Social Media Influencer: The Ultimate Guide to Building a Profitable Social Media Influencer Career

Learn How to Build Your Brand, Create Viral Content, and Make Brands Beg to Pay for Your Lifestyle

Change Your Life Guru

Books by **Change Your Life Guru**:

Affiliate Marketing Mastery: *The Ultimate Guide to Starting Your Online Business and Earning Passive Income - Unlock Profitable Affiliate Secrets, Boost Earnings with Expert Strategies, Top Niches, High-Performance Products, Innovative Tactics and Essential Tools for Success*

Dropshipping Business Mastery: *The Ultimate Guide to Starting & Managing a Thriving Dropshipping Business - Skyrocket Your Income with Proven Strategies, Profitable Niches, and Unleash Powerful Marketing Tactics*

Etsy Store Mastery: *The Ultimate Guide to Building Your Own Etsy Empire - Learn Proven Strategies for Finding & Selling the Hottest Products, Building Your Brand, and Dominating Your Niche on Etsy*

Online Course Mastery: *The Ultimate Guide to Creating and Marketing Profitable Online Courses - Learn How to Find Your Niche, Create Engaging Content, and Succeed as an Online Course Creator*

Online Freelancing Mastery: *The Ultimate Guide to Making Money as an Online Freelancer - Unlock Proven Strategies to Monetize Your Skills and Talents, Market Yourself, and Go from Zero To Success*

Online Tutoring: *The Ultimate Guide to Creating a Profitable Online Tutoring Business – Become an Expert in Your Niche, Craft Engaging Sessions, Harness Powerful Marketing Strategies, and Profit from Your Expertise in the Digital Learning World*

Print on Demand Mastery: *The Ultimate Blueprint for Print on Demand Success - Unlock Actionable Tips & Strategies to Starting, Setting Up, and Marketing a Profitable Print on Demand Business*

Social Media Influencer: *The Ultimate Guide to Building a Profitable Social Media Influencer Career - Learn How to Build Your Brand, Create Viral Content, and Make Brands Beg to Pay for Your Lifestyle*

Subscription Business Model: *The Ultimate Guide to Building and Scaling A Predictable Recurring Income Business - Attract and*

Retain Loyal Subscribers, and Maximize Your Profitability with Proven Strategies and Best Practices

YouTube Influencer: *The Ultimate Guide to YouTube Success, Content Creation, and Monetization Strategies - Build and Grow a Thriving YouTube Channel and Boost Engagement with Proven Techniques and Insider Secrets*

THANK YOU – A Gift For You!

THANK YOU for purchasing our book! *You could have chosen from dozens of other books on the same topic but you took a chance and chose this one.* As a token of our appreciation, we would like to offer you an exclusive **FREE GIFT BOX**. Your Gift Box contains powerful downloadable products, resources and tools that are the perfect companion to your newly-acquired book, and are designed to catapult you towards freedom and success.

To get instant access, just go to:
https://changeyourlife.guru/toolkit

Inside your Free Gift Box, you'll receive:

- **Goal Planners and Schedulers**: Map out manageable and actionable steps so you have clarity and are empowered with a clear roadmap to achieve every goal.

- **Expert Tips & Tricks:** Invaluable tips and strategies ready to apply to your life, or business, to accelerate your progress and reach your outcomes.

- **Exclusive Content:** Free bonus materials, resources, and tools to help you succeed.

- **New Freebies:** Enter your email address to download your free gift box and be updated when we add new Free Content, ensuring you always have the tools, information and strategies to sky-rocket your success!

Are you ready to supercharge your life? Download your gift box for FREE today! [**https://changeyourlife.guru/toolkit**]

Table of Contents

Introduction

The overarching problem is that everyone sees and uses social media from a different perspective. –Neal Schaffer

Mankind has come a long way from sticks and stones. Years and years of a long and arduous journey have resulted in the birth of what has now become a lifeline for human society—the internet. It has been proven in extensive scientific studies that man cannot thrive without society, and man's quest to connect to others has resulted in the evolution of social media today. Social media is a powerful tool that people use to find and connect. In the past, social media was largely controlled by the privileged and lucky few with either vast amounts of resources or giant corporations with the means. Today, however, social media is accessible to anyone with access to an internet connection. The people have the power to contribute, connect, and share. Social media today does so much more than just connect and share. People have found fortunes, connections, communities, and so on. Anyone could pick up a phone or any other internet-connected device and do things that were unthinkable just 50 years ago. Social media has become such an important part of daily life that to imagine a world without it today is to imagine a world of war and strife—an empty world. Social media, and the internet at large, have become resources. It has become a fundamental human right within its sphere, and with the clear influence it can possess, it is not difficult to see why.

As with all resources and power, the one that rules is king. A social media influencer today is arguably about as "powerful" as the leader of a small island or the church leader of a tiny village. It is easy to see why anyone would want to be a social media influencer, especially in the digital age of the 21st century.

An influencer is a person who utilizes social media to create inspirational, educative, or entertaining content that appeals to a group of people. They often have large followings on social media and can influence people's opinions, mindsets, dress, diets, lifestyles, and so on. Influencers are referred to by several names such as content creators, thought leaders, bloggers, etc. Influencing is a broad market, and the entry barrier is significantly low. A person might be an influencer with only a few followers. What matters for an influencer is that they can create content, direct that content to a group of people who engage with this content, and, as a result of that engagement, affect or influence people's thoughts or decisions to varying degrees.

Social media influence in itself is a term that is used to describe a person's ability to influence or affect another's thoughts, decisions, or actions. The degree to which a person can affect people's decisions through social media is directly related to the amount of influence that they control in the social media sphere. Organizations can then harness this influence for themselves by partnering with influencers to create awareness for their brands.

Social media influence does not need to be a path through suffering and tears. Influencer marketing is becoming quite an enormous sector packed with several possibilities in its developing future. Several economic, social, and cultural industries have seen an increase in their growth and popularity—a trend that may in part be attributed to the rise and growth of social media influencers. Influencer marketing is quite lucrative for influencers and effective for brands looking for anything from growth to general popularity. There are several reasons to become an influencer, and the path is relatively straightforward.

Becoming a social media influencer is less complex than you might have thought. The very first step is rather self-explanatory. To become a social media influencer, you should first learn how to create content. Being a social media influencer is largely about the content, and good content will bring good and loyal consumers, which is the goal if you are seeking to grow and become a name in the business. Creating content seems to be such a simple step, but it is also arguably the most crucial skill that a social media influencer needs. It is a factor that could make or break one's entire career as an influencer.

To create good content, you must also know what good content is. Take a long and hard look at all the pieces of media that you already consume, and take note of the ones you enjoy the most. The type of media we enjoy is mostly determined by personal differences, and good media may be said to be subjective.

Content has to pass a few checkpoints to be accepted and generally judged to be good. Good content has the following distinguishable features:

- **Original:** No matter the outlet, one would agree that good content needs to register in the minds of the audience. Original content stands out from the crowd. In today's media, due to the availability of the internet and internet devices, there is a saturation of content. Several people are doing several things, and to become a successful influencer, you need to stand out from the rest.

  Every human being on the planet is unique and has different quirks and characteristics. Those subtle and major differences in everyone can be capitalized on in the search for recognition as an influencer. Original content comes from the things that make you a different influencer from other influencers in your niche. Personal experiences, unique humor, ideas, and so on are things that could differentiate a person from others and set apart your career from everyone else's.

- **Actionable:** An indication that content is good is when it is actionable. Content should always have the goal of leading the audience to do something. This could be anything from reading similar blog posts to sharing the content with one's family and friends. Good content seeps into the minds of its readers and speaks to them. An example of this is a newsletter asking people to sign up to continue to view more content. Content should always be clear, straightforward, and actionable.

  Including social buttons or links on your page and directing the audience to it is a way to make your content actionable. Leading the audience to subscribe to something or just giving instructions about something in general is a great way to do that also.

- **Educative:** As naturally curious and investigative beings, human beings constantly find themselves answering and asking questions. Whenever content is made and shared, people will naturally come to ask questions. It is a part of existence. As a social media influencer, you should aim to soothe the part of them that asks questions. You should learn to structure your content in a way that you anticipate any questions people might have and answer them clearly and concisely.

Creators who make content about specific niches which involve knowledge sharing may find that they do this more often and have more opportunities to produce educational content that answers questions. For example, an influencer that makes videos about nutrition will find that they are constantly disseminating knowledge to the public. They are teaching and imparting knowledge to people about things that the average person might have no idea about. This will raise questions in their minds, which the influencer could then answer in subsequent content releases.

- **Accurate:** A teacher should know what they are teaching. There is a saying that goes "it is easier to teach a person who does not know than to teach a person who knows the wrong thing." It is highly impossible to fully explain the dangers of wrongful information.

As a social media influencer, you will constantly create, share, and gather content. This content must be accurate and correct for an influencer who wants to build a stellar reputation. No one likes an influencer who lies or creates content that is inconsistent with the truth. The people's trust is paramount for an influencer, and there is no quicker way to lose it than sharing lies and misinformed content. However, in today's world, there is room for everyone to fly. Some creators have become "popular" by sharing content that is misinformed. There is a special edgy side of the internet that likes that type of content. Depending on the type of influencer you want to be, this is a possibility that you might want to consider.

However, where this is not the case, you should remember to properly research your content. Crosscheck facts and properly cite sources when you have gotten the information from elsewhere. It is also important to note that credibility is highly desired and promoted on the internet, where there is a plethora of wrongful information. Correct and verified information will be sourced and promoted on search engines and other sites that cite the content.

Another key to becoming a social media influencer is to share on social media. It goes without saying that for you to become a social media influencer, you must use social media. Sharing content is how you learn to build a brand and develop a community. There are thousands of popular social media websites and applications available today. As an influencer looking to share content, you should be focusing on one or more of these platforms. Picking the right platform is also a factor that could contribute immensely to the success of an influencing career.

There are many different kinds of content today being published on social media around the world, and just as many strategies and tactics to thrive and succeed on each one. Choosing the right platform to concentrate on as an influencer is about as important as it is for a store or shop to select a good location to set up its franchise. A store that sells good food may never become big because they are located in a terrible place where people cannot find out about it. In the same vein, an influencer needs to be very particular about the platform that they choose to focus their content on.

For intellectual content, an influencer could try Reddit, Quora, or even X. These are the common websites people use today for knowledge. For content that is more business-focused, one could try Facebook or Instagram. Each social media website caters to a different subset of people interested in several different categories of media. To know which would be best, you first have to examine your goals. Understanding what you would like to achieve with your influence is key.

Another thing an influencer needs to be successful is planning. It may sound like an obvious thing to do, but it is amazingly easy to overlook it. A successful influencer must be able to create valuable content consistently to stay on top. It will only be detrimental to one's brand to release content sparsely. Commitment, dedication, and consistency are values that people love and resonate with. Displaying these qualities in your influence is highly beneficial.

Once you have decided on the kind of content that you would like to create, it is highly advised to create a calendar of content that you will release next. This helps to enmesh a sort of structure into your daily influencing activities. This also helps to keep track of one's goals and the steps taken to reach them. You will find this extremely helpful on days when the goal seems quite far away, and you are less motivated than usual. Decide how many times in a week you want to create content, and decide how often you would like to post them. You can base this decision on the results of your research on the best posting times for your content.

Engagement needs to be maximized at all times, so you need to test continuously until you find what works for you. You could also make use of Search Engine Optimization (SEO) and hashtags to improve post visibility.

As an influencer trying to gain traction, the community can often be an enormous help. This is why community engagement for a social media influencer could never be overemphasized. An engaged audience is an interested one, and this interest could then be directed as one pleases. You need to consistently engage with your audience to build a community. Without community engagement, good content is nearly useless. A creator could continually create good content, but where there is no one to see it, it remains in the dark.

Social media platforms promote content with high engagement and make it more visible to the general public on the website. There are algorithms in place to facilitate all of this. When you create content that appeals to the algorithm, you will experience an upsurge in engagement and visibility. The algorithm will reward your engagements with views, and this snowballs into more and more engagement.

As a brand owner looking to be recognized, it is important to improve one's visibility. There are several things one can do to improve their visibility and make themselves more findable. You might need to invest in advertisement, copywriting, SEO, and partnerships. Being seen is very important for an influencer. For example, a brand looking for influencers of a certain niche would likely do some research on Google to find the best influencers with the highest engagements. If your visibility and engagements are high, the chances that the brand picks you to work with are increased greatly.

To become a successful social media influencer, one must do several things with consistency and grit. Like every food has its distinct taste, every social media influencer must also know to whom they appeal. A social media influencer must be a master of who they reach, who they want to reach, and the fine space in between. Choosing a niche is one of the most important things for a social media influencer. A niche must be comprised of questions such as the following:

- What are your interests?

- What are you enthusiastic about?

- What do you love?

- What do you want the niche to be?

- What are your quirks?

- What things do you enjoy?

An athlete with an interest in bodybuilding is a natural match for becoming a social media influencer who teaches and instructs people on fitness issues, gym routines, and a general fitness-focused lifestyle. They are strengths that reflect their personality as well as their interests and expertise. The ability to truly enjoy one's social media influencing niche is part of the qualities that separate veterans in the market from newbies.

A love and passion for anything may see people rapidly developing themselves to evolve their entire lives around those things. Lots of professional social media influencers have their lives revolve around the things that their influence is about, and this can be great for influencing careers on social media.

However, too much of anything is usually detrimental in one way or another, and this might start to affect one in another area of life.

With a clear and healthy balance as an influencer, the way that one relates with the internet and social media becomes different. Things that might have been previously overlooked will now fully be in the spotlight. Things such as behavioral quirks, how one engages with the online society, engagement levels, the target audience, the posting frequency, etc., all come into view. One may notice that they are becoming more critical of these factors and paying attention more, as they are things one would ordinarily overlook. Another imminent change that one might experience is that they might start to be more conscious of the kind of content that they consume.

Creating content as a social media lifestyle influencer will allow you to understand the kind of work that goes into a lot of posts out on the internet, as well as the reasons they were made. As a content creator, you will begin to monitor what you consume to understand more about your content and your rivals' content as well.

Another likely effect that social media influence might have, is that it forces you out of your comfort zone. A regular person could get by with just being a homebody who rarely goes out and interacts with other people except when it is necessary. This kind of lifestyle would work against being an influencer. An influencer is a brand, and for brands to prosper and thrive, they need visibility. For that to happen, they will need to network and socialize a lot more often than the average person to gain and build some valuable social traction.

Participation in local, regional, and national social events will only benefit and not harm an influencer's career.

In the age of social media, things go viral all the time. Participating in contests, events, forums, and webinars will get you noticed, and one might potentially even become a trending topic on a social media platform.

As a social media influencer, staying on top of trends should be your superpower. Nobody wants a newspaper company that delivers old news. In the information technology age that is the 21st century, information is power—and whoever gets their hands on information first can control and direct whatever narrative they would want to spread for whatever reasons. Acquiring information, sharing such information to the public in a timely and controlled manner, optimizing this content for reach and engagements, and so on, are things that you will become all too familiar with on the journey toward becoming a successful social media influencer.

The perks that come with being a social media influencer are so many and cut across different parts of life. In the same way that there are several different types of news companies, there are different types of influencers as well, and the benefits that they receive vary just as much.

As an influencer who is making your name in the market, different kinds of brands will come to work with you and collaborate on some level. As the influencer grows, so do the types and kinds of clients that require their services.

Some of the benefits a social media influencer receives include the following:

- **Image**: For an influencer, image is key; how you present yourself to people, the way that people see and relate with you, the things that you relate with and talk about, the places that you go, and, last but not least, the people who you associate with. These are all important to varying degrees and may affect an influencer greatly for better or for worse. One of the first and most important things an influencer benefits from is an image boost.

  When big brands come to partner with an influencer, the influencer's image is immediately boosted. Their names will be associated with the brand's public recognition, and their image in the market is immediately boosted.

  Recognition almost becomes a currency. Famous influencers who partner with famous brands will become more famous, and vice versa.

Any respectable brand with a good reputation to protect would not risk associating itself with a public figure who could reduce its popularity or make its brand image suffer. Influencers would also not partner with brands that could potentially sully their names.

- **Flexible schedules**: One of the best things about jobs in the information technology age is that they are not entirely bound by time or location. As a social media influencer, you get to decide how you want your time to be scheduled. You plan and schedule your content calendars and travel or work to whatever degree you decide on your own.

  This career path offers flexibility that is alien to traditional job types, as you can work from anywhere with a laptop, smartphone, and a reliably quick internet connection. Nearly everyone has these things, so working across the globe is not a pipe dream; rather it is the reality of an influencer.

  There are several mothers, fathers, and industry professionals who commit to social media influencing as a side interest to their daily jobs. While most people are outside battling with traffic, heavy weather conditions, or even just strenuous physical activity, an influencer can work from the confines of their homes or offices.

- **Free products**: Depending on the type of influencing that a person does, there may potentially be several brands that would want to associate with them.

  As a popular influencer, many brands of different sizes will contact you for collaborations. Several brands send out carefully curated and customized gift packages to influencers, free of any monetary charges, in the hopes that the influencers will wear and use their products while telling their followers all about them.

  Some brands negotiate contracts with influencers to have them create periodic content about their products. Contracts are not mandatory, but they are advisable in helping both companies and influencers manage their interests. Contracts outline each party's expectations, protect the parties involved, and ensures that the obligations are met.

- **Travel opportunities**: Being an influencer is a lot of time and investment; however, when it pays off, it is largely worth it. As an influencer grows, their cooperation with other brands and people increases. In the age of technology and social media, this could lead to their fame and success in crossing national borders. Local and international brands that want to be associated with them will come calling, and this will pave the way for future opportunities.

  Some of these brands may require the physical presence of an influencer for a particular purpose, such as in-house collaborations and photoshoots, and this could mean free flight tickets for the lucky influencer. Travel opportunities are always great for influencers because of their need to constantly socialize, engage, and relate with other people and brands.

- **Community**: Developing a niche as an influencer is necessary for future growth and development. One lovely side effect of whittling down to a specific point of sale is that it brings like-minded people to the fore and allows them to connect and communicate as a community. Influencers who cater to specific niches are privy to such communities and often form the focal point that unifies these communities. Having a community is essential for several things, including but not limited to growth opportunities, partnerships, personal development, sponsorships, knowledge sharing, etc.

  Communities can help out with several different aspects of life, however seemingly unrelated they are. A common saying is "a problem shared is a problem solved," and this can only be made possible due to the enormous power that a community holds. The larger the community, the more apparent their effects.

  Communities may be seen as the bedrock of human interaction. Mankind has always sought community and companionship, and man can only truly thrive with the support and society that community brings. To be able to tap into that may even be referred to as one of the superpowers an influencer possesses.

Different kinds of brands offer many different kinds of incentives and perks to influencers. For example, an airline company working with a travel influencer may present this influencer with free trips, free souvenirs, and free merchandise for publicity purposes. A restaurant working with a food influencer may send them food packages or gift sets or perhaps even free food at their stores and shops. There are many different possibilities in the world of influencing that are up for grabs and freely available to any influencers searching for them and working toward them.

- **Fame**: A side effect of being a successful social media influencer is the recognition it comes with. Creating content that does well helps with creating a successful and well-known brand. Good social media influencers usually develop loyal and devoted fan bases just like celebrities and other famous people. This contributes to their fame and high popularity. This opens the influencer up to even more collaborations and people, and in return, even more fame.

An after-effect of fame is special treatment. Celebrities and famous people generally get offered preferential treatment wherever they might be. Perks like this range from special tickets to gifts and souvenirs for almost no reason. People will often offer gifts to celebrities as a sign of goodwill or simply just appreciation because of how much they can connect with such celebrities.

- **Money**: Influencer marketing is one of the fastest-growing economies in the world. Businesses are gaining huge returns from influencer marketing, with brands seeing as much as six times their investments. Influencers are presently highly sought after, and rightfully so. Influencers themselves are recording profits at all-time highs, with some celebrities receiving as much as $1.6 million per post.

Influencing as a profession is a rather lucrative career path, as there is always an opportunity to scale up your finances and overall income. Influencers can work with multiple brands at once, ensuring multiple streams of income for some time. Creators may earn commissions from affiliate links, royalties from collaborations, and profits from advertising and merchandising. The social media influencing market is expected to grow by several percentages as time goes on. In between the endorsement deals, the growing popularity of social media, the ever-astonishing developments in technology, and the booming influencer market, there has never been a better time to become an influencer.

There are also different categories of influencers according to the size of their following.

Micro-Influencers

Micro-influencers are the influencers with the least number of followers, or creators with a small but significant audience. An influencer is an influencer regardless of the number of their social media following. If they can generate engagements and possess the ability to persuade or affect people to some degree, then they are eligible for partnerships with marketing companies or brands.

A micro-influencer possesses a larger social media following than a regular person but a smaller number of followers than a celebrity. This figure is under 100,000. They are often the best bet for marketing companies or brands looking for a specific niche of people or a small but closely-knit community.

Macro Influencers

A macro influencer is essentially famous. They have crossed the threshold from small business to relatively big business and have the numbers to prove it. They are usually social media personalities who have a larger and broader audience than micro-influencers. They have high media values and commensurate reach and influence with people.

A macro influencer is someone with over 100,000 followers. They are generally easier to find, have more experience, and can reach larger audiences than micro-influencers. However, this often comes with a price tag that befits this level of influence.

Celebrity Influencer

A celebrity influencer is just as the name entails. A person who has reached celebrity status is known by a very large group of people and can affect or influence their decisions. Celebrity influencers have over 400,000 followers. The price range for hiring them may often run into millions as well.

Becoming an influencer is a life that many aspire to; however, a lot of people will find that without the right guidance and direction, it can be hard to make headway in this career path.

Several reasons could tempt a person to become an influencer, and in this book, we will show you exactly how to become one of the best influencers on the internet, regardless of whatever area you choose to delve into.

We will have in-depth discussions about social media influencing that will show you the common pitfalls, the dos and don'ts, the most common concerns, as well as the best ways to approach all of these from the right angle to give you the knowledge needed to be the best possible social media influencer that you can be.

Chapter 1:

Finding Your Social Media Niche

As an aspiring social media influencer, you have probably scoured all possible information sources that you could lay your hands on by now. You have read so many books, articles, and magazines, and you have been to all the crevices of the internet looking for how to become a successful social media influencer—either that or this is one of your first forays into social media influencing, and you don't know much about influencing.

If you happen to be in the former group, you would have seen several websites by now telling you that you need to do everything possible to narrow down your content to a specific niche to make headway in the influencing world—they are right.

A niche is a particular position that matches a person's talents or is very fitting for a person. It is what separates a person from another person on the internet. A niche could be anything as broad as economics or as specific as pet owners in a certain country. Narrowing down your content to a niche is a great way to establish yourself as an influencer and set yourself apart from the competition.

How to Find Your Social Media Niche

Finding your niche as an influencer is often the most difficult part that aspiring creators struggle with. There is often a lot of confusion about what to make content about and what to discuss and overall anxiety about having to pick one area to specialize in. Finding a niche does not need to be so hard. To find your niche, you will need to delve deep within yourself to find answers to several questions. You will need to be very honest with yourself to get the best results.

1. What are you interested in?

2. What do you like to do?

3. What are you passionate about?

4. What do you want people to feel when they see your content?

5. Who do you want to reach?

Once you have answered these questions, it is important to research whether there is anyone doing something similar. This will help give you a clear direction on what you want your niche to be and what type of content you would like to produce. To do this, there are a few steps you could follow.

Step 1: Find a Theme

You will need to decide how you want your content to feel to the audience. This is where you choose the direction, topic, or aspect of life that you want to create content about. This will eventually become what your brand is known for, so it is important to be thorough. You may decide to create content about food, culture, science, technology, fashion, fitness, etc. What you create content about is up to you, and no one except you should have a say in it.

Step 2: Narrow It Down Even Further

As an influencer, delving deeper into your content to find a particular pain point will never hurt your business. People often have very specific problems or interests, and in a world of 8 billion people, it can often be hard to find someone who relates. Narrowing down your message means that your content will be more likely to reach and resonate with people than broader-scoped subjects. It will often feel to the intended audience like a personal conversation, and this can have very positive effects on the eventual formation of a community.

Step 3: Research

As someone trying to become an influencer, you will need to become very comfortable with research. Researching will need to cover everything about your content and niche, as well as your present results.

Your audience, your content, your rivals, and your strategy—these will all need to be evaluated, and the results will provide data for what needs to be tweaked and what could perform better.

There are several thousand niches of content available on the internet for consumption. However, there are more popular niches in which people generally tend to have a lot of interest. Niches such as

- fitness

- beauty

- cosmetics

- health

- fashion

- animals

- lifestyle

- food

- music

- parenting

- comedy, etc.

There are as many niches as there are people interested in them, and after answering all of the previous questions, you should have a solid idea of where you want to focus your energy by now.

A factor that could affect your decision on a niche is how much money could potentially be made from a niche. Profitable niches often have large communities of people interested in them, hence they are more profitable than other niches. Depending on the type of content you would like to produce, there are different social media websites where such content would thrive and is generally more sought after.

There are rapidly growing niches that are gaining traction and inspiring new influencers and audiences. There also exist large, well-known niches that have been popular for years and years, are profitable, and have large communities.

Some of the more profitable and popular niches include the following:

- **Finance**: With the world poverty index showing that several billion people live in multidimensional poverty, it does not need much explaining when we say that everyone needs money. Knowing more about money is something that everyone needs, whether or not they know it. Blogs that give information on personal finances, saving, investments, and so on have found enormous audiences. As a blogging influencer, you might choose to write about budgeting, managing debt, money-saving tips, and so on.

- **Lifestyle**: Lifestyle is arguably the most popular niche for creators of all kinds. From blogging to vlogging, lifestyle is a different kind of beast in the world of content. Whatever we do daily is part of our lifestyle. People like to watch other people's lives as a form of entertainment, drama, or even just to educate themselves better on things they never knew. With lifestyle as a content choice, it is the people who connect to the content rather than the content connecting to the people.

- **Travel**: Travel has always been a large industry worldwide across social strata. People love to travel, and people love the new experiences that come with travel. No matter the level of technological development, travel is one thing that has followed humankind through its evolution. Due to the advent of technology and the development of the internet, people from all walks of life can now be transported into the lives and experiences of strangers through nothing but their mobile phones.

People can connect and share more than was ever thought possible. Inevitably, people began documenting their travel experiences, and it has snowballed into one of the world's largest content markets. Bloggers, content creators on Instagram, and even YouTubers will inevitably find several opportunities to make money in this niche.

- **Fashion**: Photo-sharing applications have become oddly popular in the world. Websites such as Instagram and Pinterest have skyrocketed in usage and influence, and several million people are registered on these platforms. People make use of them to do everything from discovering new fashion trends to keeping up with their favorite celebrities and their lifestyles.

The fashion niche is one of the largest industries and is constantly growing. Statistics and growth analysis research have reported that revenue in the fashion sector is predicted to become quite substantial in the future. With merely an account and content creation on one of these platforms, a person could stand to potentially make millions of dollars.

- **Food**: Food is so important that humanity could not survive without it. As our main life source, it is apparent why this niche is so popular in the world of social media. It is a topic that will continue to find popularity as long as mankind lives. There are numerous sub-niches, and information about very specific diets exists everywhere. There is information to cater to everyone, and "cooking" in particular is a favored category.

This niche is extremely populated with creators; however, it is just as lucrative to immerse oneself within this niche. There are several opportunities one could try which include writing recipes, making cooking videos, constructing meal plans, diet advice, or even just tips on using kitchen utensils. Monetization could also be done in several ways, including partnering with brands to create content using their merchandise or equipment, offering live cooking instructions from the brand's physical location, creating content while recommending the brand, etc.

- **Personal Development**: As literacy and introspection have increased in popularity, personal development and self-care have become rather important topics in recent years. People are more aware and attuned to the changes going on in their lives as well as their mental wellness and well-being. It is no longer an interesting trend but has become a serious industry as people are learning to take better care of themselves and others around them. A content creator in the personal development niche may sell digital products such as ebooks, courses, etc. They could also create podcasts, organize talk shows, or commit to coaching others and obtaining sponsorships and endorsement opportunities.

When deciding which niche to delve into as a creator, there is no lack of choices. Content is the life that we live, going to work, the food that we eat, the cars that we drive, and the pets that we own. Content could cut across every single aspect of life that we live as human beings today—the possibilities are endless, and the list is inexhaustible.

We have already established that as a social media influencer, you need to pick a niche and focus on it. However, we haven't discussed why.

Why Is a Social Media Niche Important?

Think about the last time you wanted to do something that required specific knowledge—something like learning how to cook. Chances are that you would not go to a computer center that was offering free cooking classes. To learn to cook, going to a culinary school or learning from an already established chef would be the natural decision. In the same vein, a person browsing a social media website on the internet would rather search for cooking videos from a known chef or food creator than from someone who creates content about everything and has some videos on cooking.

In case you haven't yet been convinced that picking a niche is important, here is a list of reasons why you definitely should be:

- **Minimal Competition**: Becoming a social media influencer is like owning a business. In business, there are competitors, there is competition, and the dog positioned closest to the bone is the dog that gets to eat. As a business owner looking to own a profitable business, it would be in your best interest to pick a market that has little competition.

  While it is still unlikely that you would win, it is easier to fight 10 people than to fight 100 people. In life generally, picking and choosing battles is an underrated skill that is useful throughout life. Picking a niche automatically separates you from most of the noise. You do not have to battle with already established brands and creators that have been in the business longer.

- **Expertise**: Establishing yourself as an expert is something that will continue to bring returns as a social media influencer. Experts are sought everywhere in their different areas of expertise. Experience and specialization are highly sought-after in today's world, and experts are in high demand. When you are the expert on a certain subject matter, you are the go-to person for a lot of people.

  As a social media influencer with expertise in their niche, you will be better able to exercise your options with brand collaborations and such because you would likely be a highly sought-after specialist. As an expert, you would immediately be ahead of the pack, and this is rather useful when it comes to establishing a career.

- **Profit**: It can be incredibly rewarding as an influencer to niche down, especially financially. Catering to a specific niche of people can lead to being paid more for products or services because people need your expertise. This could come from consultation, business, or any number of ways. When deciding on a niche, it can often be worth it to decide on niches with no established pioneers or competition.

By leading a new niche, you can have first pickings on everything and can pave the way for the market. Catering to a fairly new niche can be highly lucrative if it is a niche with the potential for high demand. When a problem is common, there are often large numbers of people searching for solutions. As a problem-solver in such a situation, there is no end to the possible benefits.

Becoming a Social Media Influencer Within Your Niche

There are several reasons why you should narrow down to a niche and specialize. Once you have identified a niche that you would love to create content about, you will need to explore it and become comfortable with being a social media influencer in that specific niche. There are many common pitfalls and challenges that have been faced by everyone who has begun on this path before.

Tips for Achieving Social Media Influencer Status

Here are some tips for avoiding those challenges and succeeding as a social media influencer within your niche:

Choose a Suitable Social Media Outlet

As an influencer, putting your eggs in several baskets works against the vision. It could be detrimental to you as a beginner to not focus on a social media channel to concentrate on.

One of the first things you should do is select a good social media channel that suits your kind of content and begin developing a solid presence on it. Pick a popular media outlet that has a large audience and use that to share your content.

Stay on Top of Your Niche

As a content creator, it will be in your best interest to be one of the first to discover things within your niche. People love to learn, and they will be drawn to you if you continue to post things that constantly educate them and answer their questions.

Be Authentic

Being authentic as a social media influencer helps you to stand out. The social media world of creators is saturated, and there is so much of the same content being delivered in the same way. It would be of benefit to you to try to stay away from the norm. Delivering original content that is easily recognizable as your brand will help in establishing a foothold later in your career.

Create Content Schedules

You should learn to create content schedules or content calendars to make sure that you have a well-defined timeline for content creation and advertisement.

Decide how many posts you would like to share over a given period and break down the workload. This will also help you have a more effective work plan.

Organize Your Content

Creating content several weeks or months ahead of schedule is not such an uncommon thing for influencers. On the contrary, they do this often enough that doing it seems to be the true badge that makes one an influencer. Busy schedules and occupied timelines make this an essential skill to have as an influencer.

It also helps to create enough backup content as an influencer, as you then have a ton of material to work with later and use as necessary in times of need. Other influencers have affirmed that those times come very frequently.

Devise Content Strategies

No planning at all is also a type of planning. However, this will not be very helpful to an aspiring social media influencer. You will need to search deep and choose how you want to create valuable and inspiring content, how to ensure its uniqueness, how to attract an audience, how to market your content, programs to associate with, and who to partner with.

You should have overall strategies and more detailed ones in each section of your creation. It will help set the stage for the future as well as show off your content in the best possible way to prospective consumers. You should aim to build credibility, stand out in a good way, and be relatable to whichever audience you choose to address.

Learn to be Consistent

At some stage in their lives, everyone has started something, been inconsistent with it, and eventually dropped it or stopped doing this thing completely. A successful social media influencer needs to do the exact opposite to thrive. You will need to deliver high-quality content consistently to remain in people's minds and slowly build credibility which will translate to a large following.

Social media websites nowadays are optimized to promote content that not only stands out but is frequent. Brain studies have been carried out to understand how humans pay attention and how to capitalize on it. Keeping an engaged audience at bay with consistent content will expand your visibility on social media and create more opportunities for your growth.

Advertise Your Work

While keeping an audience entertained, it is easy to concentrate and become focused on the attention it gives, and one can forget to focus on expanding the business and bringing more consumers in. You can create amazing content, but if there is no one to see it, it is no different from bad content.

You should be aware of Search Engine Optimization (SEO) to boost your visibility and reach on the internet. You will need to use strategic keywords and phrases to rank higher than competitors on search engine results and social media in general.

Create a Community

Being an influencer means that you relate with a group of people and hold significant social currency among them to affect their views or decisions on a subject. You need to remain accessible to this audience of people and to do that, this means that you will also have to relate with these people. Communities sometimes form organically without the assistance of anyone, and organic communities are often very loyal, devoted, and well sought-after.

You should try to do what you can to gather enough people who have your content in common, and then focus on creating a community from that. This means you should do things that will earn people's trust, increase participation, reward members that contribute, and encourage expansion. Communities will often form naturally when these are present.

Engage the Community

Brand growth means that at some point, you will start to struggle with communicating with a large number of people, but this can always be managed by hiring people to moderate engagement with the audience. You can start by replying to comments and questions under your posts, as well as participating in group discussions, fan pages, and so on. You should try to remain as present as possible and participate in events and forums around you. If you do this while encouraging and rewarding behaviors that foster community, the community will naturally start to grow.

Research the Competition

In the influencing industry, competitive research is something that will come in handy more often than not. Researching what others in the same business are doing is the equivalent of checking your influencing career out from another perspective. You will need to gain insight into what they are doing better than you, and what they are doing worse than you, and you will need to utilize this information to improve your content and your brand image in general.

To do this successfully, you will need to understand a few things. You will need to know and truly understand who your content caters to. You will need to improve how you advertise yourself. More marketing in the beginning stages of an influencing career would not hurt. You will also need to identify the areas where you are not doing too well and what you could be doing to patch this gap and improve. Lastly, you will need to adopt a scalable approach. You need to keep the future in mind as you grow, and directly, this ties into your brand's future.

When it comes to becoming a social media influencer, the list of best practices, advice, and tips is long-winded and extensive. However, here are a few more things you could do to try to improve your chances of becoming a successful social media influencer:

- Improve your visibility.

- Document your journey.

- Perform constant evaluations.

- Stay relatable.

- Ask questions.

- Focus on one content type.

- Involve your audience.

- Don't be afraid to specialize.

- Partner with influencers in your niche.

As you start to grow and establish yourself as an influencer, you will use these several tips and naturally start to know which of these works for you or what should be done less. You will gain a feel for what works and what does not. You will begin to form close connections with other influencers and creators, and you will learn to develop a community and establish yourself within it.

As long as content exists, there will always be people who produce it and share it. Your best bet is to be original and genuine with your content and let your peculiarities and quirks shine through. Things such as your personality, your talent, creativity, your peculiar worldview, your habits, and your preferences can all be of immense help to you on this journey.

Best Practices to Grow in Your Niche

This chapter has introduced you to the first few steps you need to take on your path to becoming a social media influencer. We have covered topics such as the importance of deciding on a niche and its advantages, the way to pick a niche, the hottest niches available across all social media platforms, tips to survive and thrive as a social media influencer, and influencer best practices.

Once you can tick off all of the items below, you will be well on your way toward becoming a successful social media influencer. It is a long and arduous journey, but with these well-sourced tips and best practices, you are now one step ahead of any competition you may have. Go ahead and use all of these wonderful snippets to start your social media influencing career on the right path.

Having already discussed what niches are and the importance of deciding on a niche for an influencer, we will be moving on to another important thing that you should know. The next chapter will be focused more on the audience that receives your messages and how to reach them.

Checklist

	Decide on what you are interested in.
	Pick something that you like to do.
	Decide on a niche that you are passionate about.
	Research properly about your niche.
	Create an account on a suitable social media website.
	Be original with your content.
	Organize your content.
	Create content schedules that have timelines for your content creation.
	Create detailed content strategies that contain action plans for your social media influencing career.
	Be consistent with your content.
	Advertise and push your content.
	Ensure that you engage the people who respond to your content.
	Develop a community of people who relate to your content.
	Reward the community that you have created.
	Participate in the community.

	Investigate the opposition or fellow competitors.
	Journal your progress and document your journey to becoming an influencer.
	Specialize your content and develop your specializations.
	Evaluate your performance constantly and tweak what needs to be tweaked to get better performance.
	Focus on a specific format of content such as audio, video, etc.
	Communicate with similar influencers in your niche and collaborate.

Chapter 2:

Finding, Knowing, and Reaching Your Target Audience on Social Media

If you have ever had business aspirations, you will probably have come across this statement several times. Content marketing advice all around the internet has this phrase sprinkled all over, and this should be enough to let you know just how important it is. Knowing your audience can make or break your entire run in a social media influencing career. It is often the sole difference between being a good social media influencer and being an exceptional social media influencer. The statistics do not lie.

What Is a Target Market?

To know how to reach a target market, we must first understand what a target market is. A target market is essentially the people who you want to spread your message to. They are the people who you have decided are the best possible demographic to receive your message or content and give the best results that you are looking for. They are the ones who are most enticed by what you have to offer and have some characteristics in common such as age, location, income levels, buying habits, content preferences, or their internet behaviors in general.

They are the ones who will relate the most to your content and share it, and they often are the ones you will need to form a community within your niche. When it comes to a target market, you can widen your net as broadly as possible, or you can specify as much as possible. You will need to perform research to know which of these to do. There is no one rule to picking a target market, and there are several possibilities available.

Defining a target market is key to better understanding your ideal customers, how to reach them, where to reach them, and how to present your content to them in the most appealing way. A great example of a target market is a specific demographic such as people born during a particular period that live within a particular geographical location; e.g., Generation Z adults that live in Korea. Getting more specific helps to target your decided market more effectively.

Defining and Finding Your Target Audience on Social Media

As a social media influencer, you will come to relate with people on a different level than normal. Doing this lets you understand that people have different preferences, and everyone cannot like everything. You will need to come to terms with the fact that you cannot sell yourself to everyone. Some people will see your content and immediately love it and share it with their friends, never forgetting how your content made them feel—and others will immediately hate your content and will forget as soon as possible. Being a social media influencer means you will have to learn who is most likely to listen to you, and how to find more people like them.

You will need to speak to them in a language that they understand and interact with them. This will make them want to interact more with you, will help them to develop loyalty to your brand, and cause them to be willingly affected by your developing influence. Identifying your social media target audience will help you to direct your energy toward the right places and focus on where your content is most well-received.

Discovering the perfect social media target market for your content is something that will continue to benefit your career for a long time. Influencing on social media without identifying a target audience is like having something to sell and not knowing who to sell to. The target audience for some products can often be very clear and unambiguous.

For example, it is common knowledge that a couple that is expecting a baby would need products centering around newborns. Items such as baby clothes, baby food, milk containers, and such are obvious products they will be on the lookout for. The target market is expecting parents, and the product is baby items.

Discovering a target market and corresponding product to offer to them is not often as simple as that. Finding a target audience on social media can be quite challenging, and some influencers go their entire careers without ever truly discovering where their content belongs. There are several data sources on the internet that provide wrong information on how to do this, as well as great sources that provide accurate information. Here are a few steps to help you find your target market.

Figure Out Who Is Currently Receiving Your Content

A great way to find people who would buy your products is to find people who are already interested in your products. One of the first steps to identifying who you want to sell to is knowing your existing customer base. Knowing who your content finds is arguably the most important step to directing your content to where you want it to go.

You will need to understand what makes up your current customer base and what interests them—you can then go on to find out what you need to tweak and find more people like that.

Gather data on who your content reaches, who responds, who does not, who shares your content, and who you would like to direct your content to. You will need to gather information such as the following:

- **Geographic location**: Which side of the world loves to watch your weird and very specific content? Where do your fans live? Understanding where your current traction is coming from is key to knowing how to target others. It allows you to have a better grasp of the time you should be releasing content, how to schedule your calendar, how to position your ads, and how to structure your content for the best visibility.

- **Age**: Knowing your audience's age can help you relate to them. Certain age demographics are more susceptible to certain marketing and influencing strategies than others, and understanding how old the majority of your audience is can help target them.

You can also target more than one age range depending on multiple factors such as buying ability, dependability, etc. Some demographics are more likely to be interested in your content than others. For example, with digital products, there is not much point in targeting older people. Most internet users would be of a younger disposition. For a digital product, you can target an age range of 20- to 30-year-olds successfully and tweak it as needed.

- **Spending ability**: This is a feature that needs no explanation. It would be unwise to spend time and effort advertising products to a demographic who don't have the ability to purchase your products or content, unless the purpose of marketing to them in the first place was not profit-driven.

Other factors include things like language and internet availability.

Find Out What Your Competitors Are Doing

As a social media influencer, the importance of knowing what your competitors are doing cannot be overemphasized. You will need to find out who is buying your competitor's products and services, as well as everything about them. This will later translate into data you can use to target a similar demographic for your career. Finding out the strengths and weaknesses of a competitor can help in finding your strengths and weaknesses.

These may also be used as starting points in developing yourself and in your future growth. It might be rather difficult to gather in-depth information about your competitor's audience, but gaining a general sense of them is often enough. Make sure to take note of how your competitors approach their audience, how they create engagements, how they interact with their audience, what they are doing best, and what they could be doing better.

Utilize Social Media Analytics

Analytics often offer deep insight into getting a clear picture of who your customers are. They help you understand who is interested in your products, why they are interested in your products, what they do with your products, and so much more. You gain immense information about who you are reaching and who you could be reaching. This will help you to understand how to interact with your consumers.

There are lots of people who could potentially be interested in your brand, even if they are spread out all over the world and have never heard of you. Analytics helps to find where they are, and you can then decide how to utilize everything at your disposal to reach them.

Define Your Target Market

Understanding what you have to offer and who exactly you want to offer it to is key. You will need to position your brand in a way that makes sure that you have a clearly defined target market and way to reach them.

You need to be clear on who you want to address and all their behaviors, quirks, and abilities. An example of things to help define a target market include

- purchasing ability

- technological usage

- education status

- social media usage

- location, etc.

Getting lost is easy when you do not know where you are going. If you have a clear idea or picture of where you need to go, getting there is less of a hassle. Having a clear idea of who you would like to address as your social media target audience will help immensely in finding them and all of the extra details you need about them.

Incorporating all of these tips will help you in the search for your ideal social media target audience. You already know that you should look for a target audience, and you now know how to find them—but we have not told you why just yet.

Why Is It Important to Know Your Audience?

In your budding career as a social media influencer, not knowing your target audience is the same as doing things without a focus. Imagine a scenario where you need to do chores on a weekend. If you go ahead and start these chores without focusing, you will likely end up starting all and finishing none. You would eventually be left with half-swept spaces, half-washed plates, half-cleaned windows, and a half-clean house. Your energy would probably also be depleted and you will have no further motivation to perform those tasks to completion. In some situations, it is helpful to be able to spread your net over a wide area and focus on many different things, but when it comes to your social media audience, having a solid idea of your target market is key.

When it comes to social media influencing, targeting the right audience is one of the surest ways to win. So many influencers suffer from targeting the wrong audience, and this in turn leads to detrimental results, such as losing potential consumers, losing current consumers, etc. Identifying your audience allows you to break them down into parts and understand which parts work best with your strategies and techniques. You should not be looking to reach everyone. Your goal instead should be to reach groups that your content will be most attractive and marketable to.

Some key perks or advantages that come with knowing your audience include the following.

Focused Engagement

As a human being, conflict is unavoidable. You cannot satisfy everyone, and some people will naturally come to antagonize and disagree with you. "Battles" and disagreements simply cannot be avoided. Some special situations will occur where you will have to disagree with multiple people. Regardless of whether these disagreements are physical, political, or simply verbal, you will need to take each opponent one at a time. You will need to focus on the most imminent threats and neutralize them while keeping an eye out for the next to stay ahead. Identifying a target and focusing your energy will help you out more than simply engaging everyone at the same time.

Knowing your target audience helps you to direct your energy toward a clear, direct, and specific place. Spreading your net will most likely hurt your chances and diminish the results of your hard work and effort. Knowing your target market, understanding their behaviors, and identifying their likes and dislikes will allow you to tweak and direct your energy in ways that are beneficial for both you and them.

Competition Elimination

Standing out from the competition can often be a difficult thing to do. Regardless of your niche, you will encounter other competitors. Separating yourself from the noise can often take tons of effort; however, one thing that could instantly give you a head start is identifying your audience. Focusing your energy on one part of an audience can often be the key to standing out. Competitors may focus their energy on the same audience you are focusing on; however, there are often subcategories within every audience.

Identifying a trait or pain point that your competitor is not addressing can help you turn the tide and bring an entire market over to your doorstep. People like to feel listened to and engaged—they like their needs met and they like to feel welcome. If you can identify what you could do to draw them in closer and tailor your content in a way that speaks directly to them, they will likely follow you over any competitors that already exist or may exist in the future.

Time Management

Time management is something that nearly the entire human population struggles with. It is a problem that has existed as long as man has. For human beings with lifespans averaging between 50 to 60 years, time is a finite resource. Being able to manage time effectively is a skill that not many have.

The more time that you spend focusing on who matters, the less time that you spend on who does not. Finding your target audience will help you manage your time better, as you are spending the little time that you have on the people who will like and engage with your content. Your time will be better spent catering to the best possible customers you could have, rather than those who would only waste your time and ultimately dampen your efforts.

Consumer Loyalty

When you find a target market to address, you have found the proverbial gold. Loyalty is an admirable trait that can often be spurred on by the most mundane things. Finding a target market that is a good fit for your type of content may feel like an ordinary occurrence to you, the content creator—but to the people being targeted, this could give them the warm impression that someone is finally paying attention to them. It could feel very much like a personal and direct conversation, and this makes people feel good—and when people feel good, they are likely to come back to what has made them feel good.

Simply creating content for a very specific group of people in a targeted market could initiate brand loyalty and in return, win you some very dedicated and loyal fans who will stick by you as your career develops.

Common Problems With Identifying a Target Audience on Social Media

Although finding your target market can be fulfilling, there are some common problems that people face when trying to reach a target audience on social media. Some of them include the following.

Unavailable Audience

One problem that content creators come across now and then is that their target audience is not on their chosen social media outlet. As we have mentioned previously, having the best food means nothing if there is no one to eat it. Creating content for a demographic that is barely on the social media platform that you have chosen is a sure way to get your content ignored.

For example, a creator creating content about pensions and investments on a platform that is mostly full of teenagers is almost automatically a lost cause. The suitable target audience for that type of content is working class and retired people. Make sure to research and understand if your audience is on the platform you have chosen to focus on.

Limited Reach

Finding an audience is one problem—being able to reach your audience is another problem. If your content is not consistent and visible enough, it will likely not reach its target audience. It is important to utilize every possible tool and strategy available to maximize visibility and reach to have your content get to its intended destination.

Performing social media analytics, paying for advertisements, and collaborating with other social media influencers can help you increase your reach and allow you to become visible to your intended market.

Reaching Your Target Audience on Social Media

Finding and reaching your target audience can be the holy grail for your influencing career. It is often what separates novice creators from established influencers. There are several ways to find and engage your preferred demographic on social media. Some of them are discussed below.

Effective Ways to Reach Your Target Audience on Social Media

- **Tailor your content to your audience**: One of the best ways to reach an audience is to let your content find them. You will need to produce content that relates to them, motivates them, is useful to them, timely, and relevant to them. Create content about the things that they like and are interested in. This is a guaranteed way to bring them to your table.

  The content that you create needs to resonate with the audience that it meets. If your content is tailored and targeted toward them, it will be easier for the content to reach them. Algorithms and complex technology around the internet constantly evaluate people's interests and recommend similar content to them. Tailoring your content to an interested audience will have these algorithms do the work for you and take your content to them.

  You can try blog posts, newsletters, articles, video content, memes, or any combination of these to get a feel for what type of media your audience likes to receive.

- **Collaborate with other influencers**: If you are finding it hard to reach your target audience alone, a great way to overcome this hurdle is to collaborate with influencers in your niche that already have the community and audience that you need. Partnering with relevant influencers in your niche can be a very powerful technique to use in the early stages of your career.

Participating in collaborations with already established names in your niche can help your content to piggyback off of their influence and help similar people in their audience to find and relate with your content. A well-executed collaboration could do most of the hard work for you and allow you to extend your visibility, grow your reach, increase your audience, and take your career to the next level.

- **Invest in advertising**: There are several options available for paid social media advertising. Paying for advertisements is a card that often pays off when done correctly and consistently. Your adverts will be displayed to several internet users at once, and the likelihood that someone watching will like your content is often quite high.

  You will need to invest in advertising with authentic brands that have advanced tools and products specifically for increasing reach and visibility. You could also invest in advertising with other influencers within your niche, thus taking your targeted advertisement to another level.

- **Utilize hashtags**: As an aspiring social media influencer, this is probably not the first you have heard of hashtags. The importance of hashtags in finding communities and audiences is immense. Ignoring hashtags will be detrimental to your goal of finding a target audience. Hashtags are often tailored to the specific communities or relevant audiences that they relate to. Using them can make sure that your content goes directly to the audiences that you intend them to reach.

  You will need to perform in-depth research on the relevant hashtags in use among the audience that you need to reach. A good tip is to link the specificity of your target audience to the specificity of your hashtags. In the way that targeting more specific niches is better than generic ones, more specific hashtags are more useful than blanket hashtags that get lost in the noise.

- **Track your performance**: While doing everything possible to become a better and more successful influencer, it can be easy to lose track of what matters and what does not. A good way to ensure that you are always doing the best you can be as an influencer is to track and record your performance. You could try all the tips in the world, but when you have no prior record of what has worked and what has not, it is easy to get stuck running circles around problems that you have solved before.

You should track and monitor your progress across campaigns, strategies, and content. Keep an eye on the subtle details and monitor what works and what does not. This will help in all of your future work because you will always have a reference board you can use to optimize and tweak things to give you the best possible performance.

There are numerous tools to use to monitor and track your progress across any social media platform you choose to use on the internet. Also, consider some paid options, as some paywalled tools offer some functionalities that others may not have available and will be of immense benefit to you.

A target audience will help you in so many ways and make your work easier as a social media influencer. Finding your target audience will help you identify the audiences that are or may be interested in your content. Content creators often go through long and trying periods of experimentation, improvising, and trying new things in the way that they approach their influencing lives. You should not be afraid to test new things and invent new things that work for you in your quest to become a successful social media influencer.

Best Practices to Find Your Target Audience

This chapter saw us discuss everything about target audiences—what they are, why you should know them, how to reach your intended audience, the importance of having a social media target audience, and the many ways in which you could reach your target audience. After reading and carefully understanding this chapter, you should have sufficient knowledge of target audiences and how you would reach them. This will be a crucial chapter in your journey toward being a successful social media influencer.

In the next chapter, we will be discussing how to find your way around modern social media platforms. We will cover how you should behave on social media, how to use social media safely, and how to build your followers step by step.

Checklist

	Investigate the audience that is currently accessing and watching your content.
	Create detailed reports about what your competitors are doing. Find out what their audience likes or dislikes about their content and their brand.
	Use social media analytics to understand your current markets as well as potential markets and consumer data.
	Be exceptionally clear about who you want to target and define your ideal target market. Do not be afraid to narrow them down to specific traits or features.
	Understand why it is necessary to have a target market, its advantages, and common problems you could run into.
	Investigate and perform all the research needed to confirm that your intended target audience is on social media and reachable.
	Use social media analytics to increase and maximize your reach on social media. This will also help you recognize and improve your weaknesses and gaps.
	Create and devise your content to appeal to a particular audience.
	Make sure that your content is relevant and useful to this target audience.
	Try collaborating with other social media influencers in your niche or a niche that you are looking to break into. This will

	maximize your visibility and connect you to your intended audience.
	Invest some money into advertising with agencies and other brands.
	Incorporate advertising with other influencers to target their already-established market and community.
	Make use of hashtags relevant to your niche and target audience.
	Try increasing how specific you are with the target audience you are targeting.
	Journal and document your journey to discovering and engaging your ideal target audience. This will help you notice gaps and weaknesses in your approach. It will also help you visualize what works and what does not.

Chapter 3:

Navigating Social Media Platforms

Many years ago, mankind used several different methods to communicate. Communication was important and very necessary for survival as a species. Man learned to leave drawings in caves that told stories of their pasts and their heritages to educate whoever was fortunate enough to lay their eyes upon these murals. Humans learned to use fire and soon began to use smoke to communicate, too. From drawings and smoke, tales would be told, and thousands of words would be exchanged.

Mankind went on to develop technology, and this technology has advanced to such levels that we may communicate with one another from opposite ends of the world without much effort. Social media has brought people together and created many communities that allow people to thrive today. People can pick up their phones and instantly speak with faraway friends, family, and even strangers.

Communicating with large numbers of people has been made as easy as making a few swipes and gestures on a mobile device. With this freedom and access, however, comes a staggering number of dangers and threats. Every day, internet users must maintain a certain security standard to remain safe on social media. As someone looking to become a successful social media influencer, traversing the internet must be done professionally and safely.

Navigating social media means that you will have to follow trends. You will have to grow your following on social media as safely and as effectively as possible.

Ways of Navigating Different Social Media Platforms

You do not have to go very far on the internet to discover several horror stories about how social media was harmful to someone. Using social media unsafely can have some very serious consequences, which is why we will be learning how to do so safely.

A few things you could do to use social media more safely include the following:

- **Scrutinize what shows up in your feed**: On social media today, you are often presented with a feed that is personalized to you based on your content preferences. You are usually in charge of your feed and can organize your content to your taste. You should remember to unfollow accounts that are known to be false news merchants.

  You should also listen to your body while patrolling your feeds. If you notice that you often feel anxious or nervous or even irritated, this is your sign to watch your content intake. Your body might be trying to tell you to spend less time on the screens.

- **Research applications before use**: Nearly every created application today contains terms and conditions for their use. A lot of times we skip them when we really should not. These conditions usually contain bits and pieces of how they intend to use data gathered from your phone, such as your application usage, your phone usage frequency, your location, and so on. They contain private details which we should be careful about exposing. Some applications are unethical and could misuse your data. You should pay careful attention to things like this, as well as the application's or website's reputation on the internet.

- **Think about what you post**: There are several million people on the internet at any given time. This is enough reason to think twice about whatever you want to post on the internet. Imagine the horrors of mistakenly posting an embarrassing picture of your younger self with a funny appearance. Even if you delete it immediately, someone might have already seen it. You should be extra careful not to reveal any personal information on social media that could compromise your security and safety. You should know that it is hard to truly achieve anonymity on the internet and it is better to be safe.

- **Monitor your social media usage**: It is easy to get distracted and fall into the rabbit hole of endlessly scrolling social media websites. This can often turn unhealthy and can cause real problems in people's lives. Social media websites make more money the more that you scroll, so they spend lots of their time and money looking for ways to make you scroll even more. Phones and internet devices nowadays usually come with inbuilt usage-measuring features to monitor your phone and application usage. Use these to ensure that your time spent on these sites is moderate and that it does not get in the way of any tasks that you need to complete.

Navigating Social Media Safely for Professional Use

Using social media professionally means that you are a brand or entity with a reputation, and you need to ensure that it remains good and professional. To use social media professionally, there are a few best practices to keep in mind.

- **Remember your reason for using social media**: You should ensure that you keep a straight head and remember why you are on social media. Understand all that you stand to gain from using social media professionally and keep this in mind when you conduct yourself. You should look to create value and remain relevant while sharing information and knowledge that helps to develop your niche.

- **Understand the different social media platforms**: Social media websites exist far and wide across the internet. There are different themes across all of them, and knowing what they are helps in understanding the way that people use them as well as the results they could probably bring. Several platforms are depending on the type of content people are interested in. Social media website types include blogging sites, video-sharing sites, picture-sharing sites, and so on.

- **Establish your brand**: You need to interact with people professionally and in respectful ways. This is what you should ordinarily do as a member of society, and it should translate into your persona as a brand on social media. Good and respectful communication will help to create a professional image of your brand in public and will help you develop a brand with a solid reputation.

When to Post on Social Media

Being a human being often means that you have busy schedules and long hours filled with things to do. Oftentimes, one of these things is using our phones. Our peculiar schedules ensure that we all use our phones at different times of the day, and according to social media analytics, there are recommended peak times to post on social media for maximum visibility and reach.

Good posting times ensure that your content is seen as much as it can be seen while the greatest number of people are online and using their phones to browse social media. There are several articles on the internet that discuss the best posting times for different social networks. While these are generally blanket recommendations and actual results may vary, they are rather good points to start narrowing down what would be the best time for you to share on social media.

What to Post on Social Media

Content on social media is often about different aspects of daily human life—and daily human life can be a lot. There is so much content everywhere that can be capitalized on, but this is often hard to spot. Deciding what to post on social media can often be a hard thing for social media content creators. From following trends to trying internet challenges to promoting educational content and showcasing one's culture—there is no shortage of ideas for what to post on social media. Here are a few tips to give you ideas on what you could post on social media:

- **Share business posts**: Think about your brand. Your brand is a business itself, and your content is a product. Creating content about your brand is a great idea for a social media post.

- **Tell a story**: Telling a story is a great way to use social media. You could break your stories up into parts and post as frequently as you want. People often appreciate art and creative works, so well-written stories would be great content as well.

- **Post about your culture**: No two people on the planet are the same. This means that everybody is different in many different ways, and we often have very interesting origins. Talk to people about the different things in your culture. Show off your culture and teach people about things that they should know.

- **Share niche content**: You can create content about your niche to share with audiences around the world who enjoy your content category. Instead of writing typical and generic things that already saturate the internet, you could write or share videos about things specific to a particular group of people.

- **Share product reviews**: Consumerism is the order of the day in the 21st century, and people are ordering and using new products daily. You could find some new products to try every day and post about your personal experiences using these products. A good example would be posting phone reviews or new application software such as games.

- **Share advice**: Rather than create another long tutorial showing people how to do something, you could share tips about something that you have encountered. Tips and advice about doing a specific activity are often highly watched content on the internet, and there is a huge audience out there waiting for you.

- **Share funny pictures or video memes**: Everyone needs a laugh now and then, and the people who contribute to making everyone smile are cherished on the internet. Meme pages are a huge market on the internet and have attained growing internet popularity in recent times. Accounts on the internet have hit as high as millions of followers from just posting hilarious content for people to laugh at. Even companies and corporations post memes with their official accounts. This is a niche that can be rewarding to specialize in and has the additional perk of making you smile and laugh as you work.

- **Post about your personal opinions on popular topics**: Opinionated content creators are always going to be fun to watch for the average internet user. People giving their honest perspectives on several issues can often bring in a lot of viewers with the same views or opposing opinions, leading to discourse and internet debates.

- **Create content about free resources you have found**: Free resources are in high demand all over the internet, and people often share tips on how to get them. A good example of a free resource you can share is promo codes for stores or food discounts. People are constantly looking for these types of content and are often grateful enough to reward the posters with their following—sometimes in hopes of getting more useful free resources.

- **Post job openings and opportunities**: Unemployment is rampant in the world, and helping unemployed people get jobs can feel very fulfilling. What better way is there to create great and popular content while also helping humanity out? Posting timely information on job openings can be rewarding in more ways than one.

- **Talk about history**: History is a topic many people are interested in but often find too boring or convoluted to settle down and dig into by themselves. Creators who offer bite-sized bits and pieces of important historical facts and figures can become quite popular, as they are providing knowledge and offering value to people at no extra cost.

- **Talk about nutrition**: Fitness and health and all their related topics are very good content choices when choosing what to share on social media. With a lot of people taking their health more seriously, a lot more people are interested in nutrition and healthy eating. You could take it a step further and curate diet plans for people's different body types and different weight goals.

- **Share posts about the food you have tried**: Food is great content, whether it is cooking videos or kitchen tips or even just videos of yourself eating food. There is something that connects people to food, and making content about it is almost always a good idea. If you have an extensive or rather specific diet, you could make posts about your food and its nutritional or psychological benefits.

- **Create informative "how-to" videos**: Humans discover new things every day. New information is constantly coming to light about everything that people do and different new ways to do them. People are gaining lifelong skills and expertise from watching internet videos and practicing.

  You could share videos on skills that you have and how to do them. You could teach people with informative content showing them what to do step by step.

- **Create product reviews**: Creating reviews about products from a certain niche is a great idea that you could try. Brands are constantly on the lookout for favorable reviews from popular brands and people. They often reach out to influencers with collaboration and sponsorship deals that could improve their image to the public. Pick interesting things around you to make reviews about, such as electronic gadgets, clothing items, restaurant food, etc.

There is so much potential content out in the world. There is no harm in being authentic and original or even a little weird—it all adds a little spice to the pot of soup that is your content. Struggling with content topics or post ideas is natural. Here are some more ideas for content you could post on social media:

1. Discuss community content.

2. Create a weekly series on a particular topic.

3. Share jokes or comedy content.

4. Make content about tourism.

5. Create content about your art.

6. Post flashback pictures and videos.

7. Talk about the latest movies. Share reviews about movies you have watched.

8. Post client testimonials.

9. Share reviews about songs you have listened to.

10. Share about your journey through your career.

11. Post content about you learning something new.

12. Talk about other people's content that you like.

13. Share content about you interviewing someone.

14. Post daily tips on a niche topic.

15. Make daily posts about items on your bucket list.

16. Create informative content about social issues.

17. Post about holidays.

18. Share throwback content.

19. Talk about common mistakes people make.

20. Share hidden features of things that most people never knew.

21. Post about fashion.

22. Discuss sustainable development goals.

23. Make content about success stories.

24. Share freebies and free tips.

Following Trends on Social Media

It can be quite hard to stay on top of everything that social media throws at you, especially if you have other commitments. The world is constantly changing, and staying afloat on new developments can often be an entire job by itself. As a social media influencer, you will need to be aware of the latest trends in the media, and you will need to participate in some of them to stay relevant and deliver fresh content to your followers.

What Is a Social Media Trend?

Trends are popular behaviors that people follow and copy for different lengths of time. Social media trends are things that become increasingly popular among a group of people usually for short periods on a social media platform. Trends develop every day and are forgotten about almost as quickly as they spread and become viral on the internet.

As a budding social media influencer, it is rather crucial to stay informed about social media trends, as these are usually great opportunities to become very popular in short periods. Social media is a moving train. Things that were in fashion yesterday may not be in fashion today, and monitoring the changes that occur allow you to identify great expansion opportunities.

Ways to Follow Social Media Trends

There are numerous ways to keep on top of social media trends and stay afloat in the digital world. Some of them include the following:

- **Do your research**: Sometimes you can find trending topics on social media websites simply by searching. Trends have become a normal thing on social media today, and some applications and websites have gone as far as having dedicated trend pages for anyone to see what is trending at the click of a button. Download popular social media applications and play around with hashtags. You will stumble on a couple of trends.

- **Check news feeds**: Some social media trends end up becoming popular enough that they often end up in traditional news outlets and informative articles. Scouring news feeds for the latest trends is a great way to find trends and discover things that could become trends and give you the upper hand in the industry.

- **Follow other influencers**: You are probably not the only social media user trying to stay on top of trends. Other influencers are also trying to remain relevant and stay on top of information. A quick shortcut to staying on top of social media trends is to closely follow other social media influencers. Some of them will likely find great trends before they become popular, and you can join the early wave simply by following them.

- **Listen to podcasts**: Podcasts are great alternative news sources for finding out trending topics on social media. They often hold recording sessions and shows about hot issues and trends. Join and listen to the hottest podcasts available and pay close attention to the content they produce and the various topics.

There are hundreds of ways to keep things hot and fresh while following trends. A few others you might want to try include

- following other social media experts

- participating in social media communities

- checking out "What's Hot" on popular social media websites

- searching for popular keywords and keeping an eye out for recently searched phrases

How to Build a Following on Different Social Media Platforms

Having a lot of social media followers can be life changing. Notifications blowing up your phone, people always mentioning your name, several potential clients lining up for a collaboration in your messages, great social influence, and so on—the list of possible benefits is long and desirable. Getting many followers is something you will want to do as a budding social media influencer.

Simply having lots of followers is a great source of internet street credibility and clout; however, these numbers often do not add up. Influencers sometimes have several thousand followers that barely engage or share their content. It takes hard work, effort, consistency, and a little luck to build strong communities of fans that follow you and engage with your content. The painstaking work it takes to do this can often be worth it.

Here are some things you could try to help you gain superstar followers that engage and share your content as a community:

- **Host community events:** People hold online community events on social media every day. They are great ways to boost your following and drive engagement. People get to participate in contests and other opportunities while enjoying your content. This can be an excellent way to get people to follow you and subscribe to your content. Examples of community events you could host include giveaways, trivia, guessing games, highest-liked post competitions, etc.

Do things that fuel participation and drive people to band together as a community with you being the unifying factor. Make sure these sessions are interactive and personal for everyone present and reassure both participating and non-participating members that they have value. If nothing else, this will increase the likelihood that they come back for more of the same. This will contribute immensely toward your community building and following in general.

- **Use videos:** Videos are watched and engaged with more often than any other type of media. Eye-catching visuals combined with good soundtracks and audio can often hold people's attention for inordinate amounts of time. They increase engagement and grab people's attention more than other media types. Invest in a good camera and audio recording equipment for high-quality video and audio recording experiences that bring people back for more.

Marketers generally realize the importance of video as the most preferred and valued type of content on social media. Videos are shared more often than any other type of content, and quick clips hold dominance over longer videos in capturing the attention of viewers on the internet. Ensure that your story feeds and reels are full of quality video content.

- **Update your profile information:** One of the first things that people do whenever they come across strange social media profiles is to open them to check out their details. As an up-and-coming influencer, you would most likely not want to be caught unprepared for thousands of people viewing your profile after a successful content upload.

Make sure that your social media profile details are updated and ready for prying eyes. Your profile pictures should be clear and sharp-looking professional pictures of you or your work. Ensure that they fit and that all your profile details tell a story about your great personality or work.

- **Explore interviews and presentation opportunities:** Brands, local media outfits, podcasts, and news outlets are constantly on the lookout for the next hot thing to interview. As someone looking to build a lot of followers, this is an option you should look at exploring. Interviews allow people to meet previously unknown individuals and become familiar with them and their brands.

  You will get a chance to display your charm and unique characteristics before a large crowd that will want to look you up and know more about you. Actively search out opportunities to speak to people and accept interviews. You can also use the opportunity to advertise your brand and link your social media pages as well.

- **Avoid buying followers:** This is a pitfall that many social media influencers fall into in a bid to speed up their growth and look like they are bigger and more popular than they are. This can often work detrimentally, as the difference is often clear upon further inspection. Most of the bought followers are often robot accounts that do nothing except increase the follower count. They do not engage or share content and are only there for a visual effect.

  Buying followers is banned by some social media platforms, and when it is noticed, the results range from account bans to suspension upon notification of suspicious activity. It is always better to rely on growing followers organically.

- **Use data analytics:** One of the best and quickest ways to gain more followers is by examining the data from your account and using this to design a plan of action. Using data analytics helps with gathering important information that you can use to make better choices and improve your social media performance. Several applications and websites offer good data analysis tools that you can use to better understand your online footprint and how to utilize it for better results and views.

The data could consist of what type of content currently performs best with your current audience, which time is the best for maximizing views, who your content is reaching, the location of your current viewers, and so on.

- **Ensure that your content is entertaining:** It seems like this would be an obvious way to gain followers, but this can also be quite hard to do as an influencer. Sometimes some niches have content that a lot of people do not naturally find as entertaining, especially people who have not really discovered that content niche yet.

  As an influencer, you should look to make your content as entertaining as possible to whoever might be watching, even if the content is inherently mundane. Check out other creators' content and make a note of the content that you find interesting. You could make a note of the things you find interesting while watching and try to replicate them within your own content.

Other methods you could try include

- engaging in different online communities.

- participating in online contests, trends, and other relevant events.

- sharing pictures and interesting visuals.

Although videos are generally more sought after on social media, it does not mean that images do not have their own place as well. Videos are moving pictures in the end, so it makes perfect sense that images are the second most viewed type of content on social media. Sprinkle images all over your content and watch your engagement and following go up.

You could try using images that illustrate whatever it is that your content is about. Infographics are also great, as they are generally educational images. Use your creativity to merge high-quality videos, pictures, and text content to increase your following.

Best Practices for Navigating Social Media Platforms

In this chapter, we have discussed how to navigate social media. We went into the many different ways of staying safe while browsing social media, and we talked about how to navigate social media professionally. We went over the best times to post on social media as well as numerous content ideas for what you could possibly post if you ever find yourself needing inspiration or simply a content mood board. We broke down social media trends, why they are important to an influencer, and how to follow them. We also discussed different ideas that you could try to build a following on social media.

In the next chapter, we will be discussing content creation and how to create enjoyable and valuable content. We will discuss content strategies, their importance to a social media influencer, and how to create some effective social media strategies for the best results in your brand's growth.

Checklist

	Monitor your social media usage.
	Scrutinize the content that finds its way to your social media feed.
	Inspect applications and their terms of usage before using them.
	Reaffirm that the information you are sharing is not sensitive.
	Keep in mind your reasons for using social media.
	Know and understand the uses of different social media websites and applications.
	Communicate with people respectfully while you establish your brand.

Research the best time windows to post content on various social media websites.
Ensure your content is entertaining.
Use social media to tell stories of interesting things that have happened to you.
Share product reviews of products you have used. Tell entertaining stories about things you have bought and used and talk about how you feel about them.
Share your personal opinions on popular or trending topics in the media.
Use your social media accounts to post funny pictures or videos that you have seen on social media. Funny content makes people feel good and is always a great content idea.
Understand social media trends.
Perform research about social media trends.
Follow other influencers in your niche to stay on top of social media trends.
Check out popular content on social media to find out what is trending.
Host community events to increase your engagement and help you build a following.
Upload more video content types to gain even more engagement.
Ensure that your profile information is complete and up to date.
Use a current picture of yourself or your brand content to promote your content and increase your following.
Use data analytics to understand your account data and use it to maximize your following.

Chapter 4:

Creating Valuable Content

With the consequences of borders and distance growing year by year, social media has become an important tool for communication. Social media has become accessible to large populations of people around the world, and people of all ages use the internet to share different types of content between and among themselves. Different types of videos, pictures, and audio flood the internet daily. Social media has become a tool for advertising and displaying all sorts of topics, posts, and content all around the world.

As a social media influencer, the importance of good and valuable content cannot be overemphasized. Sharing quality content has helped creators amass large numbers of followers across various social media platforms. People love to read and watch well-composed and exciting content on various topics that cut across their daily lives. It is essential as an influencer to create and share quality and engaging content.

Creating Content for Social Media

Content can come in several forms, and with each separate form, there are many different ways in which you can create amazing social media content for your niche audience. Some include the following.

Blogging

Blogging can be writings, photographs, or other types of media that individuals can use to share a variety of things, ranging from conversations to personal experiences and differing opinions. Blogging is usually done by individuals but can be done by corporations and companies. Content sharing is important in today's world, and even large companies have seen its uses and advantages to their reputations and businesses. They are easy to set up and can be used to grow careers and brands from scratch.

Blogging is a great way for an influencer to grow their brand by sharing valuable content with consumers around the world. You can blog about anything you think is interesting and use well-researched marketing techniques to increase your reach as far and wide as possible.

You can use your blog to

- **Answer questions**: Every professional today was once a learner and struggled with one thing or the other. As someone learning to be a social media influencer, you are probably struggling with some things more than others. It is always great to think about what you yourself have struggled with and use your pain points as a reference to answer questions from people engaging with your content.

- **Create an informative series**: Informative posts that teach useful things are always in style. They can help to increase engagement and grow careers in very simple ways. A lot of content that teaches people things today is made into teaching series that last for a period of time. A great example of a teaching series you could create is a series talking about the top 10 movies you have seen in a particular genre.

Champion Social Causes

Humanity as a society band together really well, especially in cases where there are adversities or challenges. Social causes are great at bringing people together against injustice and unfair treatment. If your content reveals you taking a stand against popular vices or injustice, there is a good chance that it will be shared and promoted.

Simply speaking up for social causes is a great way to create content for a niche audience that is interested in social injustice, human welfare, and similar topics.

Other ways you could create good content for social media include

- creating and sharing informative content on podcasts.

- interviewing and questioning other influencers.

- discussing popular social media trends.

- creating tutorials and informative content.

Good content is always in style, and people who share good content are always in high demand on social media today. Here are a few tips for creating some of the best possible content on social media.

Tips for Creating Good Content on Social Media

- Go for niche gatherings and seminars in your industry. Read updates about new ideas, trending topics, and other interesting things.

- Create well-recorded videos that communicate great content with your audience.

- Share detailed and knowledgeable infographics that teach people new things about a chosen topic.

- Utilize influencer marketing to work with and leverage other influencers' content. Creators that share good content become recognized for good content, and this will be expected of whatever they share. Leverage this to get your content seen by audiences that love good content.

- Share creative photos that convey deep emotions and inform people about whatever you want to share.

- Craft neat and well-written copy. Make use of captions and posts that capture attention to direct readers' attention toward your other content. Good copy is always a great investment, so do not be afraid to spend a little for the best copywriters that will take your content to the next level.

- Create a detailed content calendar that helps you manage your posts and structure your content. These may run for as long as you are comfortable planning for, whether it is a month or a week. Having a content calendar can help on the days when you run out of content ideas or are too busy to record new content.

- Measuring your results can be great to maintain awareness of your engagements and reach on social media. By understanding the things that you did best and the things that you could have done better, you have effectively set up a plan for your future growth.

- Share the results of your research about something particular that you are interested in. Document and share your personal experiences and things that you found interesting while researching.

- Examine your content. Look deeper into your content data and understand where your work is directed. You might discover that you require better writing, better delivery, or even just a better image. Use your understanding of the content that you enjoy, to create a good overview of your content.

- Monitor your promotional content. Too many adverts can turn people away from potentially good content. It can be very off-putting to be constantly redirected away from good content by distracting adverts and promotional content. Ensure this is in good ratio to your delightful content.

Content Strategies on Social Media

What is a social media content strategy? Social media content strategies are comprehensive plans for the goals that you hope to achieve with your content, how you want to achieve them, and all the fine details in between. It often contains highly detailed plans that display what type of content you want to share, how you want to share it, and when you want to share it while managing your resources in the most efficient manner in order to reach your target audience in the best possible ways. The advantages to having a social media strategy are innumerable, with some of the best ones being that

- they help you to establish and increase your online presence across social media platforms.

- having a social media content strategy will definitely help you to stand out from the competition with detailed plans of action optimized to promote your career.

- it helps you to target members of your audience with personalized and tailored content for niche communities.

- utilizing content strategies will help you track and understand your performances better, allowing you to improvise, strategize further, and adapt.

Content strategies allow you to document your goals for being on social media, your tactics, your key performance indexes, as well as your progress on social media. They are highly invaluable to being a social media content manager and allow you to clearly define responsibilities and goals specific to each platform that you are trying to develop.

An influencer such as yourself might set specific goals such as raising awareness and reach of their brand, or perhaps simply increasing the sales of a product that they are selling. A content strategy will help you keep track of such goals and eventually help you achieve them in the long run. They are the master plans that ensure that your message gets across to your chosen audience in the way that you want it to.

Social Media Marketing Strategies

Marketing in social media is often an entirely different ball game from what you are probably used to. It capitalizes on how to bring in the most monetary returns from any social media campaigns that have been executed. Social media marketing strategies are a little different from social media content strategies because marketing takes your social media career to be a business and looks for how best to market your content to other people on the internet to maximize profits and make the best of your marketing endeavors.

Although social media content and social media marketing strategies are separate terms, they may be used interchangeably.

Why Is It Important to Have a Social Media Content Strategy?

With social media becoming so accessible to everyone in the modern times we are in today, businesses and individuals around the world have realized that this medium could potentially increase a brand's efforts by large percentages for little to no extra costs. Simply having a content strategy for managing your social media business could set it ahead of your peers by leaps and bounds.

Monetary reasons, political reasons, personal reasons—whatever the reason, the power of utilizing content strategies on social media cannot be denied or overemphasized. There are several reasons why you need a content strategy or two on social media. A few of them are described below.

- **It saves time and effort**: When you use social media without content strategies, it can often be very draining on your time and energy while frustrating you at the same time. You become accustomed to doing things by way of trial and error, and this is not only ineffective but also archaic and not an intellectual thing to do. Content strategies can help you to better understand the various types of content and media that thrive in your industry, as well as the likes and preferences of your target audience. They also save the time that may be better used on top of all that. They allow you to relate to your audience on a deeper level that is relevant to their wants and needs. You are able to push your content directly to your potential clients without exerting energy unnecessarily with less fruitful methods and endeavors.

- **Augmented audience targeting**: Different products means that there are always different and more ideal audiences where these products could end up. Products and content exist in harmony and create a whole new level, which many social media influencers and users alike are unable to reach with traditional methods of marketing. When performed optimally, social media content strategies allow you to send your content directly to the doorstep of whoever is interested in your products, or who could be interested, and help you better understand what makes up these groups of people and how to reach even more of them.

- **It improves and monitors your consistency**: In the influencing world, social media can often feel very unfamiliar even to avid social media users who have been active for years. New pieces of information are constantly flying by, and new market techniques are being developed every single day. When you don't have a content strategy, your content may seem disjointed, random, and unpleasing to the eyes.

With a strategy, your feed will not confuse your audience because you can closely monitor the tone and mood of your content. You may create consistent and patterned schedules that increase how relevant, relatable, and reliable your content is to consumers.

- **Content curation becomes easier**: Whether you record all of your posts by yourself or your content niche involves you reposting other people's content and ideas—content creation is made much easier with content strategies. With plans and directions in place, you can now rest a little easier with your content creation efforts. Things like running out of content or creative blocks become things of the past. With content to reference and a plan to execute whatever your creation might be, you now have a wealth of resources and tactics to choose from to determine how you create and market your content.

You end up freeing up time, and content-making becomes a lovable passion due to how easy it becomes. You are able to focus individually on all of the many aspects and categories that exist in social media content creation. Whether your goal is to increase your reach or maybe even just increase the number of buying customers within your present audience—it becomes easier to pick and choose your battles as well as understand the purposes and reasons for your content choices.

In order to craft the perfect social media content strategy, you'll need to be aware of the answers to some questions that will eventually form the basis of your strategies. Where the answers to this question are not decisive and clear, it is likely that your social media content strategy will fail. Some of these questions include the following.

- **What is your reason for creating content?** Your reason for creating content, or the why, can often be such an important factor in your strategy. You will have to decide whether you are simply creating content for creation's sake, or there is a different and particular reason behind it. Your reason could be as simple as wanting to sell and market a product, or something entirely different, such as increasing your social media reach or creating soothing content to teach and educate a particular demographic on an issue that you have identified. Reasons can often be either very specific or broad.

  It often ties in with your reasons for being a content creator in the first place. Any reason you have for creating content is valid, but put some thought into this and be sure of your decisions.

- **Who do you want your content to address?** You will need to have a clear picture of the group or subgroup of people you want your content to reach. You have all the freedom to decide, and you can be as specific or as broad as possible with your decision. You could decide that you want to reach people between the ages of 21 and 35, and you could be more specific with that selection by deciding you want a subset of that group that has access to funding through work or some other endeavor.

  Deciding who you want your content to address could be as simple as looking at your product or content and visualizing who would most likely listen to or watch your content the most. Paint a clear picture in your mind of who you want to reach.

- **What is your desired content niche, style, and format?** There are many types of media content available on the internet. Whether it is pictures, videos, or even audio, there is a market for it, a niche where people enjoy that type of content, as well as a social media platform where that type of content thrives and is shared the most. You will need to perform in-depth research on which platform is the most suitable for your type of content, as well as which place has the highest number of viewers of that particular type of content.

  Picture-sharing websites are so plentiful on today's internet, with some of the most popular being Instagram and Pinterest. If your content is mostly visual in the form of pictures or videos, you would most likely be looking for a similar platform.

- **What do you want your content to achieve?** You might want your content to simply bring more people together as a community, or you might want your content to increase your engagements. What you want your content to achieve is up to you and ties in closely with the reasons why you are making content in the first place. Keep in mind that they are not the same thing and may often be confused for one another.

  The reason for creating your content simply refers to your motivation for creating content in the first place, or possibly even why you have decided to become a content creator.

  What you want your content to achieve, on the other hand, could be something as specific as inciting public anger about a topic like climate change or trolling someone on the internet.

- **When would you like to share your content?** People use different social media at different times, and this often plays a humongous role in when social media influencers decide to post content. Deciding when you would like to share your content is a crucial part of social media strategies. There are several information metrics that can be found on the internet with details about this. These metrics are often decided by things such as the age of the demographic, their most used internet devices, the times that they get up from bed, times that they go to sleep, the most likely times they would pick up their phones for either work or leisure, as well as things like their buying capacities and occupations.

The various things that come together regarding when to post is an information sector that has not been completely understood by experts; however, it can often be very important to a social media influencer's career. Use information available to you from various news sites to gain a clear understanding of when you would most like to share your content to gain audiences on the internet.

There is a host of other factors to consider when gathering information on how to tailor your social media content strategies. Other questions that could contribute include

- What image do you intend to portray with your brand?

- Which platforms would you use to disseminate your content?

- Which social media platform would be most effective for your content style and audience?

- Who currently receives your content?

- What story do you want your brand to tell?

Creating social media strategies does not have to be so difficult. Ensure that you have clear pictures of your answers to each of these questions, and do not be afraid to get a little specific. After answering these questions, you will most likely have a foolproof base for creating your social media content strategy.

Crafting an Effective Social Media Content Strategy

Making effective social media content strategies can be quite hard and confusing with the wrong resources. It is possible to waste years and years on social media strategies only for them to be ineffective if you do not know your way around how to craft them properly. Here are some steps to crafting effective content strategies on social media.

Define the Goals of the Strategy

Social media content strategies begin long before you ever make or share the first post. Whether you realize it or not, it is involved in every facet of how you approach social media as a professional. Before creating social media accounts or posting any content at all, your strategy should already be in place. In order to know whether you are succeeding at your strategy or not, you will need to define what it means for the strategy to be successful. Your strategy will need a goal so that any positive or negative feedback in an unintended direction would not give you false aspirations. The goals of your strategy have to be in line with your goals and objectives as a social media influencer.

A strategic goal is a specific thing that you would like to achieve over a particular period of time. An example of this is aiming to double revenue over a period of two years. They allow you to define your success by key performance indexes. Some of these goals could be each of the following:

- **Expanding social media presence**: Your goal could be to become more recognized socially as an influencer. As a new influencer, this is a rather common goal to have and is a great strategy goal that focuses on increasing your brand's awareness and the discoverability of your business and social media pages. Social media reach and presence are directly tied to how well-known a social media user is, and are a determining factor in how many followers a user has.

- **Increasing engagements**: An audience could be present but not participatory, and changing this is often a big problem in the world of social media. Getting an audience to follow an account is one thing, and it is usually a more complex one to get them to actively participate and engage. Due to how common a problem this is, there are even specialists who focus on this one part of social media nowadays.

Getting more people to like your content, comment on your posts, share, or view your content could be a great example of increasing your engagement as a strategic goal.

- **Increasing your audience**: A successful social media influencing career is often determined by a large social media following. Increasing the number of people in your audience as active consumers of your content can often be a social media strategy goal. As an influencer, increasing the number of people in your audience is never a bad thing. With an increase in your audience, you stand to directly gain an increase in your opportunities and growth as an influencer as well.

Define Your Target Audience

Defining your target audience is such an important part of social media influencing that it ties in directly with every single aspect of it. Your target audience on social media needs to be clearly defined to work perfectly with your social media content strategy. You can have a clearer idea of who this is by examining your content, your products, and the data from your social media accounts. To further ease this process for you, you could install data analysis tools on your websites or social media to help track your visitors and narrow down your target audience.

You will be able to get information such as

- your viewers' ages

- their interests

- their locations

- their genders

- their activity rates on social media

- their most engaged content types

This is only possible if you already have existing social media accounts or websites, as all this information is gathered from already-established data that is generated or recorded from your accounts. If you do not already have accounts, however, you may try more traditional methods such as customer reviews and targeted surveys.

Pick a Platform

Picking the wrong platform to share your content is one of the worst mistakes to make as a social media influencer. It takes you away from so many opportunities and causes your content to underperform no matter how good it is. When you have a clear picture and image of who your target audience is, it becomes easier to decide where you would like to share your content. As an influencer, one of your targets will most likely be a sample audience that likes to spend time watching content on the internet. You will need to find a social media platform that readily has this particular demographic as an audience.

More than one social media platform could have this, along with other benefits or disadvantages which you may discover. It is best, however, to pick just one major one to focus your energy and attention on. Later in your career when you have started to become more comfortable with the world of social media influencing, you may then push to expand to another social media platform, depending on your needs or as you see fit.

Define Your Performance Metrics

If you do not monitor your content, you will most likely not know if it is doing well or not. Your strategy has to have a defined set of metrics that you would need to track to determine whether or not you are performing well. All content that you create has metrics that may be harvested, and your overall brand has its own metrics. You will need to investigate and track all of these for the best results.

Your metrics may include things such as the number of clicks on your content or website in general. When you link your content somewhere, this refers to the number of people who click these links and end up on your website or social media pages. Another metric may be your engagement levels. Tracking your engagement levels is always a great thing to do in social media strategies, as they allow you to see the effectiveness of your present campaigns. You may also wish to track how your hashtags are performing. Using hashtags is a core part of social media influencing, and tracking your hashtag performance metrics may allow you to see which hashtags are underperforming and which could be better fitted for your brand and campaign as a whole.

Other things you could include in your social media strategy are to

- ensure that your content is set up to be entertaining and engaging.

- define your content calendar and schedule your posts.

- evaluate and tweak your strategy periodically to improve performance.

Best Practices to Help You Enjoy Content Creation

In this chapter, we have seen how content creation can be rather burdensome and stressful. We have also seen how frustrating it could get if you are following the wrong steps without proper guidance. However, using all of these tips here will ensure that you have an easier and more enjoyable time in your content creation.

Checklist

	Use blogging to connect and reach your niche audience.
	Answer questions with your blogging.
	Create informative series that teach people new things.
	Utilize your blogging platform to bring attention to social issues.

	Read important developments about new topics and ideas that are relevant to you.
	Share good quality videos packed with good content with your audience.
	Use influencer marketing to utilize other influencers' reputations and communities.
	Make well-written captions and posts that hook readers' attention.
	Examine the content that you share and analyze the weak points that you need to strengthen.
	Design a highly detailed social media content strategy.
	Understand the importance of using content strategies on social media.
	Decide why you want to create content on social media.
	Define who you want your content to address. This could be a specific demographic.
	Picture the type of content that you plan to create clearly.
	Choose social media, websites, and applications to disseminate your content.
	Make a plan for when you would like to share your content to gain the best possible reach and engagement.
	Clearly define the goals you want your social media strategy to achieve.
	Examine who you want your target audience to be. This could be dependent on variables such as age, gender, or location.
	Emphasize what defines the success of your social media content strategy. This will help you monitor your progress.

Chapter 5:

Branding Yourself as a Social Media

Influencer

Social media has made personal branding and reaching people easier, faster, and less stressful. From the comfort of your home and with the right device in hand, you can go to great lengths in the social media world to identify with people, known and unknown.

Who Is a Social Media Influencer?

Whenever you think about social media influencing, your mind may immediately go to celebrities, models, and public speakers on Instagram and other social media. However, social media influence is not limited to this scope alone. A social media influencer is someone who controls the buying habits of individuals by uploading content on social media platforms. They are people who influence the choices of others to maximize sales for certain companies, establishments, and businesses.

Social media influencers in the eyes of the populace are people with perfect lifestyles, dress sense, and interests whom they think should be emulated. So, in short term, they are the modern-day gods or superheroes. They make use of this ability to make a profit for themselves and for the companies they work for.

These people are people who have built a reputation over time for themselves because of their in-depth knowledge, specialty, and expertise in a particular field. So, whenever this person pops up, what comes to mind is the field they specialize in. These people live through their field, they look at it and influence people. For instance, Rihanna is an influential figure who empowers women to love themselves. She is perceived to have a sense of style. Over the years, she has been identified as a fashion-forward and stylish person, and she has built trust with her followers in this field, thereby earning the ability to influence their fashion choices. Businesses with similar goals to an influencer make deals with them to promote their businesses and in turn pay them.

It is not far-fetched that humans are drawn to flashy things, perfection, and trends. The more a person is in tune with these things, the more love and affection they get from people; and love, they say, is the greatest virtue. People would do anything for the things and people they love and hold dear, even if it means paying for it. It is on this idea that the notion of being a celebrity thrives.

Imagine logging in to your favorite social media and you see a post about your idol promoting a particular skin product. You hear them rave about how effective it is, and it occurs to you that this product may just be the solution to any number of skin issues you may be dealing with.

That example is of a scenario where an advertisement meets a need. Often, people are moved to take action on an ad because they've been presented with the same or similar promotional content multiple times. Other times, people make purchases because the product or service was promoted by their cherished celebrity. Case in point: the previously described idol selling skin care products.

Interestingly, this idol may not necessarily be a real-life person. Say you have a three-year-old niece who will leave whatever she is doing whenever she hears "Coco Melon" on TV. Over time, Coco Melon will be elevated in my niece's mind to be more than just a cartoon but a real interactive character.

Now, assuming we go to the department store to get her cereal and she sees pictures of Coco Melon characters on the cereal boxes, that automatically becomes the best cereal in the store!

These days, everyone has a social media account, and technology has made the world into one big community where one can just swoop in and out. Social media is useful to different people for different purposes; some to kill boredom, some to talk about their business, some to connect with loved ones, some for the laughs, and others in pursuit of solutions to their perceived problems. The first thing about business is about finding out the needs and then making a product to satisfy that need and in turn making lots of cash from it. Where a community of people meets daily and interacts, it is only normal to take advantage of that medium to maximize profit.

People have different meanings for who a social media influencer is. Brown Duncan in his book, *Influencer Marketing: Who Influences Your Customers?* defines influencers as well-connected sets of individuals who have active minds and can create an impact; he also identified these people as trendsetters.

Social media has made the influencer work very easy, and by acquiring the right skills to make the most out of each social medium, you could become a social media influencer. Some people think that being a social media influencer is about having a substantial number of followers on your social media account. But the truth is, one can have thousands of followers, yet they have no influence over them, while a person with far fewer followers influences every person who follows them. Their followers are active, so it is difficult to measure a person's influence on social media. This is why it is important to harness the requisite skills to optimize social media.

Social Media Optimization

It is not enough to have a social media account and post every day to become a social media influencer. To be an influencer, you have to go to lengths to acquire the requisite skills needed to attract customers who will pay you for the services you offer.

What Is Social Media Optimization?

These are strategies used by businesses and organizations to promote awareness of their brand. It can also be defined as the use of social media platforms to grow a business's presence online.

Since time immemorial, social engine optimization (SEO) has been the standard for digital marketing. Although SEO and social media optimization (SMO) serve a similar purpose, SEO increases visibility and creates the website traffic, especially on Google. On the other hand, SMO has gained better ground in increasing a company's visibility in the online space by directing the audience from social media space to the company's website directly. Platforms that can be used for digital marketing include Facebook, Snapchat, Instagram, X, YouTube, etc. It is up to social media influencers to know how to manipulate these tools into generating income for themselves and visibility for the brands they are working for.

Certain messages can be designed in a way to influence a specific group of people on social media. For instance, the use of social media to customize business/marketing content based on age, demography, and sex is why most times you see tampon ads with women and ads for cold beverages in countries or demographic settings with hotter temperatures, etc. These are all influenced by Social Media Optimization.

Benefits of SMO

In a nutshell, these are reasons why your brand needs SMO.

- It makes sure that your brand gets a strong presence online.

- It creates a wider reach to niche organizations.

- It helps to increase social media ranking with its combined efforts with SEO.

- It is a great source for generating traffic online.

- It is useful for lead generation.

Moving ahead, one may ask how they can make use of these SMO tools. A step-by-step guide has been put together below to help up-and-coming social media influencers to learn, in simple terms, how to make use of social media optimization.

How to Optimize Your Social Media

#1—Know What Social Media Platform Is Best for Your Brand

The first step in building a brand for yourself online is knowing what social media platform is relevant. With the advent of social media networking, there are so many platforms one can use to connect with people, and there are many more to add. Sometimes this creates a divide and confusion on what platform is best for your brand. Going ahead to create an account for everyone you come across is not a wise move. This is because not all of them are sustainable; rather, more efforts should be put into creating quality content for your brand.

Choosing what platform best suits your brand can be a tad difficult; however, the following are what you should consider before deciding what social media platform to start with.

- Your target audience should be your priority, and knowing what platforms they are mostly on can help in your decision-making.

  o What is their age bracket?

  o What content do they enjoy?

  o Are they working? What kinds of jobs do they do?

  o Are they usually online?

  o At what time do they come online?

- You should set your mind that you're trying to build a community. Setting up a community and building trust and friendship with them is a good way of converting followers.

This knowledge will guide you in knowing what social media site is best used for those in your target audience.

#2—Edit Your Bios

Your bio is the first thing a person sees when they stumble on your social media page. What your bio says and how it is written says a lot about you and determines if they will follow you or not. Knowing that your bio is your first point of contact with your audience shows how serious it should be taken. Make sure your bio is straight to the point and as clear as possible. Your bio should have your business name, what services your business offers, who you are and what you do, and the topics you're interested in. Remember to keep your bio short and simple, because no one has the time to read an essay or your life's history. Keep it short and straight to the point.

#3—Know When to Post Content

The secret to social media engagement is not just posting frequently or always having content to post, but knowing what time to post this content for your followers to engage with. As the saying goes—it is not how far but how well. You have to find out when your followers/audience are mostly online, and determining this requires some hard work. You could make use of a reliable online scheduling tool with a feature that determines what time is best to post online content. Having done that, you could take advantage of it by monitoring when your followers are most likely online, post content, and boom! The engagements follow. Hootsuite is an excellent example of a platform through which brands can effectively manage their social media accounts.

#4—Use Valuable Keywords

Just like in SEO, keywords are just as important in SMO. Chances are, your target audience does not know your brand, so they will most likely not come online to type your name. What they would do is type the services they require and check out the first few accounts that pop up. So, how can you compete favorably with other brands? By researching relevant keywords for your brand. So how exactly can one know what keywords are relevant?

- Think like them. Knowing that your brand was made for people, satisfying those sets of people is paramount; therefore, you should put their interests first. Think like them. What are they interested in? How can you help them with their needs? What are their service providers?

- Having this in mind, while creating content, you have to know what words your audience would most likely search with. Here are the factors you need to determine a relevant keyword:

  - its relevance

  - search volume

  - competition ranking

  - Return on Investment (ROI)

  - searcher's intention

  - trending topics

  - location

#5—Know How Much to Post Per Day/Month

Some people have the mindset that the more you post, and the more people see your content, the more your brand registers in their minds. But have you ever thought that maybe people might just find it irritating that your business is always in their faces, and you keep bombarding them with content nonstop? You might end up losing followers if you keep up with that mindset. For one to build a brand, they have to be discreet about the number of posts they put out—a little here and there will be enough to hook your audience. Here are some patterns you could use to control how much you post on each social media platform:

- On Facebook, consider publishing as many as three posts daily.

- On Instagram, consider publishing as many as seven posts weekly.

- On X, consider publishing as many as five posts daily.

- On LinkedIn, consider publishing as many as five posts daily.

Bear in mind what time your audience will be online to see the posts you make every day.

#6—Write Engaging Headlines/Captions

The skill of copywriting comes in handy here. Remember, do not copy captions from somewhere else and paste them under your posts, as it is unethical. Write captions that will hook your audience and make them hungry for more. Do not bore them with bulky writings that lead to no end; rather, write catchy and engaging captions. You should also bear in mind that captions are social media based. A caption that is suitable for YouTube might not be suitable for TikTok, and the sooner you realize that, the better your brand will be. Not everyone is a skilled writer—agreed. If you do not wish to go through the hurdles of learning copywriting, you could hire the services of one to handle your social media posts.

#7—Use Relevant Hashtags

Hashtags are very vital for people searching for things online. You would notice that in some posts, hashtags are longer than the text on that post. They are regarded as the building block of digital marketing on social media. To increase your visibility and get to a wider reach as a social media influencer, the need for hashtags is very important. They should always be in your bag of tricks for a wider reach. More than anything, it is important for you to use relevant hashtags. Here is how to do it.

- Learn from social media influencers. Find influencers who are related to your brand niche and see the kinds of hashtags they use. If you find it difficult to choose what hashtags to use, you could check out Orbit Media Studio's guide to finding influencers.

- Some social media platforms provide users with trending hashtags; for instance, X. This goes a long way to pull traffic to your content when you use them.

- It is important to keep the hashtag short and simple. Avoid bulky words which may be confusing.

- You could find a unique hashtag that resonates with your target audience; something short, unique, and catchy.

- Make sure the hashtag you use is relevant to your brand; if not, you will be getting visibility but that which is lost to your target audience. Or you might end up promoting another person's brand in a bid to use popular hashtags.

#7—Make Use of Engaging Images

As they say, monotony kills interest, the same way overloading your audience with text content could derail their interest in your brand. Think of creative ways to engage them, such as catchy images. People are moved by what they see, so using engaging graphics could keep your customers glued to your page. Make use of pictures, memes, videos, tutorials, infographics, etc. Making sure that your content is appealing visually could help you more effectively optimize your social media accounts.

#8—Exploit Social Media Analytics

Having applied so many social media optimization techniques, one needs to monitor their progress. How well has it worked for you? In what areas do you need to improve and in what area do you need to continue? Identify the difference between the time you weren't using a tool and when you started using them. How well did it work?

Instagram has this tool to show business account users how far their content reached, how many visits they got to their page within a certain period, etc. This could help you monitor your progress online.

However, different social media platforms have their unique ways to track engagement, such as counting likes, how many times a post was shared, and how many retweets and comments were made. Tracking your progress will help you find out what works for you and how to improve to garner more engagement.

Not having a requisite social media strategy has been a problem for some companies. The lack of good strategy is one of the reasons why businesses lag when it comes to the social media world.

To save your brand from this, you will require a unique social media optimization strategy with fixed objectives; a unique strategy that will emphasize the growth of the company. With the right strategy in your box of tricks, you have the chance to stand out in your field and make excellent improvements.

Having seen the importance of Social Media Optimization tools and a few techniques that would be helpful to your brand, it is important to forge ahead with how you can brand yourself as a social media influencer.

How to Brand Yourself as an Influencer

When creating a brand, you should note that you are also creating a reputation for yourself. Your goal should be to market yourself and make sure your voice is heard, even in an already saturated market.

Here are a few tips on how to make waves for yourself and brand yourself as an influencer.

Know Your Niche

This should be the rule in any business. You have to know where you belong and identify with it before thinking of building a brand in that niche. Your niche could be fashion, sports, beauty, empowerment, etc. Because let's be honest with ourselves; there are so many experts in different areas of life.

The fastest way to discover your niche is to think of that thing you love doing, something that comes naturally to you and that you could do at any time. Now, narrow that down to a field. What is that? The thing that comes to your mind is your required niche. Now, you stick to it, gain expertise by practicing over and over, and gain skills and experience in that field.

Make sure to stick to your niche. It is very tempting to try to add other things simply because you find them catchy and you feel people would like them, too. Know that when you do not identify a niche, you stand a chance of confusing your target audience with what exactly you specialize in.

Maintain a Unique Brand Voice/Image

Maintaining a defined persona on your social media platforms will enable your followers to look up to you as one who is trustworthy and solid. Like it was mentioned before, trust is key to branding; people will only make deals with people they trust. But in a situation where you are untrustworthy and inconsistent, you stand the chance of losing your potential audience.

Finding that unique voice for your brand takes a lot of hard work to achieve; however, you have to update your profile across all social media platforms to have the same voice to ensure consistency. Now you might ask, how exactly can you do that? Here are a few steps:

- **Create guidelines**: As a brand influencer, you have to establish a set goal and focus for your brand. You could put it down on paper, in your diary, or somewhere you would see it often. Having put it down, make sure to follow it.

- **Integrate your social media platforms**: By integrating all your social media platforms, you could post the same content that cuts across this platform, thereby maintaining the same voice. An instance is a link between Facebook and Instagram.

- **Avoid using different profile photos and colors**: When all your social media platforms have the same profile photos, it screams consistency. More than that, when you use the same color scheme, it shows uniformity, uniqueness, and professionalism. People want to follow accounts that have all of these.

- **Being Present on relevant Forums**: More than integrating or using similar color schemes on your social media platforms, you have to be true to your brand. A way for you to be true to your brand is by being at the right place at the right time, such as being in and contributing to forums and organizations that have similar goals to your brand. Speaking about your brand and showing up has a way of dragging people's interest to you and what you have to say.

Following these steps creates the audience's perception of your brand. What people perceive when they engage your brand may build or mar your business. This is why your reputation should be steadfastly positive.

Import Your Contacts

You would be amazed at the number of people you know on social media platforms. Those on your contact lists may well be your audience, and surely, some of them are your target audience. You could import your contacts from your phone book, Gmail, or Outlook into your social media platforms like LinkedIn, Facebook, X, Instagram, etc.

Your Posts Should Be Positive

What you post reflects you. People who do not know you can only have an idea of who you are through the kind of content you post. Reputation is very important in the influencing market. What do people know you for? Giving off negative vibes and energy? Or giving out positive energy? All of these can be traced through the kinds of posts you make.

A better way to approach this is to think of the resume you present when looking for a job; you see how finely and meticulously written it is? You should apply the same energy to your social media posts knowing that what you show people forms an extension of you. You wouldn't like to be tagged with negativity, right? This goes a long way.

Study Influencers

At the mere mention of the word "study," people frown and sigh. No one likes to study. You might think that studying ends in school, but that is not true. You need a bit of it out here in the business world. Only here, you're not studying to perfect your grades, you're studying to be successful, to stand out, and be useful.

Before you are so many successful influencers who have achieved heights you have yet to. Studying how they started, the things they did, and their methods is an easy way to start as your own brand influencer. Also, you have to connect with these people, interact with them, and at the same time study them.

An example of a social media platform where you can come across experts in your field is LinkedIn. Here, you can observe their strategies, their posting habits, and the kinds of content they put out there.

Take a Social Media/Marketing Course

No person is a custodian of all knowledge, which is why every day we should be ready and open-minded to learning new things. Social media marketing is something you know little to nothing about, so it would be beneficial to learn from people who are grounded in this field.

There are a lot of courses both online and in bookstores on how to go about marketing online. These authors give in-depth insight into their experiences on their journey as online marketers or influencers. You could buy any of these courses and tune in to their stories.

You could also learn the basics and the ins and outs of social media, as well as what to do to send your unique voice or message to the public.

Join Active Social Media Forums

No man is an island; hence the need to socialize with people around you, those who share similar interests and focus as you. This is also an important tool to improve your brand as an influencer.

There are so many groups on LinkedIn and Facebook that offer solutions to this. All you have to do is find a forum that is in your field and join it. Try as much as possible to be active in these groups, as this will help ensure your growth in the field you find yourself in. This is why it is important to stay true to your niche.

Having seen how you can build your brand on social media, it is important to know how to guard this brand because it is your sweat and blood. There are a lot of people out there who look for easy means to make it on social media, so they steal brand names and make a profit from them. These people are called cyber thieves, and you wouldn't want what you've worked so hard for to be stolen by them. The next subtopic focuses on how one can protect their brand.

How to Protect Your Brand

Social media influencers should not be oblivious to the fact that their content can be stolen at any given time, where all they have been working for goes to enriching people who do not deserve it. Just as much as you protect your physical property from getting stolen, in the same way, social media influencers should guard their content. This is your intellectual property, and efforts should be made to ward others off. Below are a few tools that could be used to ensure your brand's safety.

Trademark Your Name

If you do not have a website with a domain name, you are at risk of losing your brand name to someone else who could start making profits off your name. You do not want that to happen, right? This is why it is important to trademark your name. This ensures a kind of security for your brand. Your brand name is your intellectual property, and you have to safeguard it by registering your trademark. That way, people cannot infringe on these rights given to you.

Registering your intellectual property (IP) is crucial to protecting your brand. Having a strong IP will go a long way in making the removal of infringing posts much easier.

Since the rules that guide the use of intellectual property have changed due to the power given to us by social media to be publishers and share content, IP on social media has become complex. Therefore, influencers should follow these rules to protect their intellectual property:

- Influencers should create policies regarding the types of use they permit as well as the ones they do not permit.

- Make use of digital watermarks on your content to keep people from stealing from you; also make use of the copyright symbol, "©".

- Use a monitoring tool such as Google Alerts that can help monitor your content.

While trying to protect their content from getting stolen by others, influencers should also make sure they are abiding by the same rules.

- They should obtain permission and licensing from brands before making use of their content.

- They should understand that promoting products falls under commercial activities and not under the fair use of copyrighted content.

- Influencers should also exercise caution before registering a domain name simply by checking if it is similar to an already existing brand.

Controlling Your Social Media Pages

You must have a page on major social media to prevent people from impersonating your business. With your presence on those platforms, there will be a significant difference between what is original and what is not, since your page will be at the top of searches.

Another way to distinguish your page from counterfeit pages is by getting verified on social media platforms. This can be achieved by applying to the appropriate bodies, and it is not dependent on the number of followers you have.

Make sure that your page includes a link that directs your followers to your various official pages. This link may be placed underneath your bio. Doing so will help people to know which pages are authentic and which are fan or scam pages. It would also inform them about your various platforms.

Read the Terms of Service

Social media influencers must read and understand the terms of service for each social media platform they use to post their content. This is because there are certain terms of service that give a platform the ownership and control of content uploaded or posted there. Some websites allow users to own the content they post on them. Without reading the terms of service, one may fall prey to losing their content to these social media platforms/websites. Knowing these will guide social media influencers on whether or not to upload their unique content.

Two-Step Verification

A secure way of protecting your content on social media platforms is by using the two-step verification tool. Here, a code would be sent via email or SMS to verify that it is truly you signing into your account. A lot of social media accounts have been protected because of this tool. If the hacker cannot access the code sent to you, they cannot get into your account and steal your identity or intellectual property.

Use Strong Passwords

Use a unique password for your social media account. Before choosing a password, think hard about something people cannot easily guess. Some people use their birthdays, which is not always advisable because it just takes a person who knows your birthday to hack your accounts. Some social media platforms and websites play their role here when they suggest to users that they make use of letters, characters, and numbers to form a strong password.

Best Practices to Protect Your Brand

In this chapter, you've learned how to not just create but also see yourself as an influencer and manage your social media brand optimally. The days when spending too much time on social media was seen as unproductive behavior are long gone. Today, you can create wealth and network with high-value personalities from various parts of the world simply by establishing yourself as an influencer.

By using the information in this chapter, you will successfully optimize your social media accounts to reach more of your target demographic and gain a large following. You will also be able to protect your accounts from hackers.

Now that you're growing on social media in leaps and bounds, you might be considering cashing in on all the work you've done. In the next chapter, we'll see viable strategies to make money on social media.

Checklist

	Make sure your social media accounts are optimized to reach a broad audience and attract the right followers.
	Always read the terms of service. Do the same whenever the terms are updated.
	Protect your account with a solid password and two-step verification.
	Establish your personal brand in your area of expertise.

Chapter 6:

Monetizing Your Social Media

Influence

Isn't it amazing how one can make money out of their influence on social media? Social media has gone beyond just interacting with loved ones and reaching out to friends. These days, you can also achieve financial freedom if you have an active social media account and influence. With the increase in the population of users on social media platforms, companies have long since brought their businesses online. Others have also opened online shops where they can easily sell their products in return for cash.

By creating relevant content with massive reach and followers, content creators/social media influencers can now monetize their presence more than ever. Being aware of these opportunities can help social media influencers learn how to leverage their new-found fame. Now, what exactly is social media monetization, and how can social media influencers monetize their brands?

What Is Social Media Monetization?

This simply means making revenue from your audience on social media platforms. This could be through the digital products one promotes in the form of affiliate marketing or the content one offers in the form of online courses. It is called social media monetization because you make money out of social media platforms.

Aspects of Social Media Monetization

There are various ways through which a person can make money online, and they include the following.

Affiliate Marketing

Affiliate marketing is a form of advertising where a company compensates publishers for generating traffic to the company's products and services. These publishers are known as affiliates, and the compensation (in monetary form) encourages them to keep driving traffic to the company's product. Amazon makes this scheme popular by creating a program in which bloggers attach links to Amazon pages for any reviewed product in exchange for fees when a purchase of the product is made. This is one of the most popular forms of making money online, and a lot of influencers keep hopping on it.

Affiliate marketing in simple terms is promoting other people's or company's products and services in exchange for a commission for the sale you make on that product. Affiliate marketing is a modernized version of an old idea, which is getting a commission on every sale, only this time around, it is digitalized. Social media influencers who have built trust with people or their followers take advantage of this to make income for themselves. For instance, bloggers who have, over the years, built impressive brands that are trustworthy can easily convince their followers to buy products from the company with which they are affiliated.

How to Become an Affiliate Marketer

Follow these guidelines to become a successful affiliate marketer:

- **Choose the product you want to promote**. As an influencer, you have to invest your time in researching the product you would like to affiliate with. Most times, they are products you already know and like, and they have affiliate programs. In this case, these products have been tested and are trusted by you, so they are easy to recommend to other people. You also know the ins and the outs of the product as well, though other times this might not be the case. In a situation where you do not know products in your niche, you could opt for an affiliate program and find out about this product. You have your reputation, credibility, and trust at stake here, so make sure you do a good job at it.

- **Get set up as an affiliate**: You have to apply, provide the necessary information, and get approved before you can start earning. It doesn't matter if you are part of an affiliate network or you work directly from a merchant. After you provide your business and personal information for tax purposes and your bank details where your commission will be paid, your affiliate merchant will provide you with an affiliate link through which your customers can make purchases. You'll then be given tips necessary for marketing the affiliate products. These include a guide, banners, sidebar graphics, and sample email.

- **Promote your chosen affiliate offers**: In order to get conversion rates, you have to get your buyers to trust you. Now, how can you do that? It comes with a lot of hard work. You could do either of the following:

  ○ Create a resource page on your bio. They are like recommendations that also show buyers how to use the products and why they need them.

  ○ Create and promote custom content.

If you would like to learn more about affiliate marketing, why not take a look at our book, *Affiliate Marketing Mastery: The Ultimate Guide to Starting Your Online Business and Earning Passive Income?*

- **Comply with legal requirements**: By complying with regulations, you show how credible you are. The Federal Trade Commission in the USA requires that affiliate marketers tell their customers that they earn a commission from selling a product to them. Although some people do not comply with this, it is good business for you to be transparent with your buyers.

Brand Partnerships

Brand partnership, like the name, entails a partnership between two brands. The brand partnership helps the brands involved to add value to their products and services. It also helps to increase visibility, reach a wider market, boost awareness, and open up new markets for the companies involved. The brand partnership is usually between two non-competing brands.

With the decline in television viewership, most companies have realized that the best way to get their product to a targeted market is to increase brand awareness and increase engagement through collaboration with social media influencers who have built their reputation and community online. As a content creator, you could make video content, graphics, blogs, etc., for other brands, and in the same vein publicize your brand for a wider reach. These brands pay social media influencers for these adverts and strike deals with them.

Ways Influencers Can Partner With Brands

1. **Media kit**. This is also known as an influencer's CV. Your media kit should contain all there is to know about your brand. Brands can summarize all there is to know about an influencer by going through their media kit. Your media kit should contain as much information as possible—your business niche, experience, expertise, previous collaborations, and successes. Do not try to narrow it down or be humble about it. It is what you do, so own it! The more impressive your media kit is, the more chances you have at landing cool deals with big brands.

2. **Pitch for paid collaboration**. This is a modern-day hunt. The hustle is real for even social media influencers.

   - Send emails and direct messages to brands.

- Make sure to introduce yourself in a professional manner to be taken seriously.

- Ask if there are collaboration opportunities.

- Talk about your experience briefly and summarize your audience demographic.

- You could send some of your content for them to evaluate how you can display their products to your audience.

- Getting an agent can be of great help. They serve as middlemen for influencers and increase their chances of landing great deals.

3. **Make sure to ask the right questions**. What is your value as an influencer? Does this deal align with it? Does the partnership feel natural to you? What is the payment scheme? Does it align with your content, or does it downplay you? Note that if the deal is not good enough for you, you can always walk away. You are free to choose who you wish to partner with.

4. **Learn how to negotiate with brands**. Negotiations are very important when it comes to business partnerships. This is when influencers and brands put their heads together regarding the terms of their contract. During negotiations, you should know your worth, be meticulous and firm about pricing, approach it professionally, and provide a breakdown of your rates.

5. **What to include in your influencer agreement**. Terms of the contract, mode of payment, and usage rights—take note of their website, advertisement, and paid social ads and ensure your payment fee aligns with the usage of rights. Your terms of payment should cover how much you would charge for your work. If your contract specifies endorsement disclosure terms, you should follow a local disclosure guide on how to go about it.

6. Having closed a deal with a brand, you have to **disclose your collaboration to the public**.

Approaching Businesses for User-Generated Content

Most times, customers who are extremely happy with the result they get from a product will share with their friends, social media followers, and family about how satisfied they are. They take a picture of the product and make posts about their satisfaction and recommend that other people use the same product and have a life-changing experience. This, in other words, is called user-generated content. It is just as the name says: content that is generated for brands through users. Sometimes brands ask for it; other times, it is done organically by users to show appreciation or excitement.

This is one of the most authentic and low-cost forms of marketing. When these brands come across this content that they are tagged in, they beam a smile across their face and they repost this content on their pages. As a brand owner, you must seek the permission of users before reposting their remarks. Now, how can influencers take advantage of this? Influencers should always seek opportunities to show up. The following is an example.

How Influencers Can Take Advantage of User-Generated Content

User-generated content varies. It could be a picture or video of the product, a video of you unboxing the package, or a casual snapshot.

- Be creative. As an influencer, creative is like a middle name. Make very creative videos, snaps, and content for specific products and posts.

- Make them notice you. Tag, tag, tag, and tag again. Ask your friends to tag the brand in your comment section, as this will most likely drag their attention to your post.

- Use TikTok. This app is slowly becoming a metaphor for viral content, as the app has made a lot of content popular through recognition on social media. How creative you are with your content increases your chances of being retained as an influencer for a brand. So, if these brands are impressed with your content, they could meet with you for another contract.

- Go for Engagement. Seeing comments, likes, and mentions of your post signifies success. The more engagements you have on your post, the more likely you are to get deals.

Creating Online Courses

As established earlier, every influencer has a niche. This niche shows that you are dedicated to your field and that you are well grounded, so people will most likely listen to your advice, quotes, and remarks regarding that niche. So why not create a course? Being an influencer in a particular field is equivalent to being a teacher in a field. This way, you have the trust of people because they have seen over time that you have advanced knowledge when it comes to your field and they look up to you. Whatever you say is like law. So, creating an online course in that field and making money out of your knowledge is another way you can generate income as an influencer.

Step-by-Step Guide for Creating an Online Course

1. Choose a topic: This is the first step. What is it that you are passionate about teaching? Once you have discovered it, put it down on paper or type it—whichever is most convenient for you. Ensure that you have in-depth knowledge in that field. Most times, it is easy to teach something we love or are passionate about.

2. Does your topic have high demand?: Do not make the mistake of thinking that your course has competitors in the market before doing some research and writing it. No one wants to make a product that no one will use.

3. Create compelling learning outcomes. Learning outcomes are important because they tell your readers what the course will teach them. Learning outcomes also explain the benefits and rewards your reader will get from reading your course.

4. Select and gather course content: This includes your research and all the necessary information you need for your course.

5. Establish an outline for your course: This helps you beat procrastination and enables you to use the information you've learned from a given topic to write your course. Outlines serve as a guideline and ensure the smooth flow of writing.

6. Delivery technique: No one would spend their money on an unengaging or boring course. So make sure your delivery is top-notch and relatable to your readers.

7. Pricing: Fix a suitable price for your course.

8. Advertise: Tell the world about it. Blow your trumpet. Promote it through your social media accounts, with friends and family, etc.

Selling and Promoting Your Own Paid Products

Promotion is key to making massive sales. Most times, promotion fails because the product does not have good quality. Although this isn't the case for every influencer, it should be a consideration, especially when you have monetized your following with sponsored posts or affiliate offers.

What you have to first consider are your audience's wants. What is it that they demand the most? For instance, if you are a fitness influencer, you could create your product by using your knowledge and skills to make protein powder, weight loss products, and energy drinks. For a fashion influencer, you could open a fashion line, and for a skincare influencer, you could open a skincare line. Selling these products would in turn earn you money.

Remember, you already have an audience that trusts you and is ready to buy the products you offer. Now you can promote these products on your social media accounts and place ads for them. For instance, Instagram and Facebook have the option for sponsored ads that can help boost your visibility.

An online course is one of the many services you can sell online. If there is a topic you are passionate about, why not create a course? Our book, **Online Course Mastery:** *The Ultimate Guide to Creating* *and Marketing Profitable Online Courses*, will help you set it up and promote it!

How to Sell Your Products Online

- Create a shop online. There are so many platforms where you can sell your products online; for instance, Shopify, Bonanza, Amazon, eBay, etc. Create an account with them, go through the necessary formalities, and post your products there. Your shop link should be in your bio so that people who stumble on your profile page can easily access it, browse through it, identify what they want, add it to their cart, and pay.

- Promote your products using sponsored ads on Instagram or Facebook.

- Create content with your product and post it on your account.

- Market your products by utilizing video format.

Sponsorship Ads

Sponsorship is a verified way of monetizing your social media. In a sponsorship contract, the sponsor or brand gets to their target market by endorsing an influencer who gets paid in return for their services. Sponsorships are highly recommended for influencers with a defined audience. This would make it easier for brands to know who to pitch to so that they will get to their target audience. For instance, a fitness brand should go for a fitness influencer. Having a massive following adds to your value as an influencer, but knowing how to convert them into paying customers is key.

On Instagram, there are two types of sponsored posts—the ones where brands pay Instagram to promote them and the ones where brands pay influencers to make ads for them/promote their business. Both are good, as they serve the same purpose of taking products/brands to an even wider reach.

Instagram made a special feature where an influencer can tag the brand they have a partnership with. It is usually indicated with "Paid partnership with *brand's name*" just beneath the influencer's username.

How to Get Sponsored Posts on Instagram

- Define your niche.

- Understand your audience.

- Post consistently.

- Make use of hashtags.

- Tag the brand on your posts.

- Remember to add your contact info to your bio. It could be your website, email, or phone number.

- Pitch for paid sponsorship.

- Charge according to your worth.

How to Create a Sponsored Post on Instagram

- Work out the scope of sponsorship and agree on the price for it. It could be in cash or kind (free sample products) from the brand. Depends on your agreement.

- Set up brand sponsorship on Instagram.

- Follow the brand's guidelines.

- Before posting, inquire of the brand whether they are okay with it.

- Upload the sponsored posts:

  o For feed content: Click on the button called "advanced setting" and choose your preferred business partner.

For stories: Follow the same action. This time around, to tag the brand, you have to click on the link on the toolbar.

Digital Ads

Digital advertising is a form of online marketing that promotes products to target audiences through the internet. It increases awareness of your brand and motivates buyers to connect with your brand. Small businesses make use of digital advertisements to capture new buyers, since it puts their brand on the customers' radar.

Other benefits of digital advertising include giving you access to unlimited data. Through this, one can gain insight into buyers' demographics to understand who they are without second-guessing.

Influencers can take advantage of this and gain money through digital advertisements by offering services such as

- content writing

- becoming an SEO expert

- affiliate marketing

- selling consulting services to companies

- working as a social media manager

- taking advantage of YouTube advertising and becoming an ad partner

Joining Creator Funds

Creator funds are a monetary fund for creators encouraging them not to leave that particular platform to join another one. TikTok introduced this feature in 2021 to share monetary funds with creators who are killing it on the platform. According to TikTok, they created the fund to "encourage those who dream of using their voices and creativity to spark inspirational careers." Isn't that exciting?

Although it is not available to all countries and is limited to the US, UK, France, Germany, Spain, and Italy, the fund pays users based on the number of views they get on content. Statistics show that you get 2 to 4 cents for every 1,000 views, which looks pretty low from this data, but if you know your way around TikTok, you could earn massively from this opportunity. You should bear in mind that TikTok is only encouraging young creatives, and this is in no way a paycheck or an ad revenue payment like YouTube's AdSense. TikTok has not been open about how they go about their payments, but users who meet their requirements are compensated with the monetary fund.

Requirements for earning from this opportunity include being at least 18 years of age and being a TikTok user in the countries where it is available.

Other requirements include the following:

- You must have a pro account on the TikTok platform.

- You need to have at least 10,000 followers.

- You should have at least received 100,000 views in the past 30 days.

- You should be following TikTok's community guidelines as well as their terms of service.

- Your content has to be original.

How to Join TikTok Creator Fund

Once you meet the requirements for the application, it is easy to apply for the fund. If you do not have a pro account on TikTok, you can set one up by going to "Manage Account" under settings and clicking on "Switch to Pro Account." The Pro account helps you track the performance of your videos.

Having set up a pro account, go to "Creator Tools" under settings. Click on the "TikTok Creators Fund" button to confirm your age and agree to their terms and agreement. Then the wait begins. If TikTok accepts your application, you're good to go.

Selling Leads to Other Brands

Learning how to sell leads is an extremely beneficial skill. "Leads" are potential customers who are yet to be convinced to make a purchase. Being able to identify this category of customers and introduce them to other brands gives you an avenue to advance your business and at the same time allows you to help brands that are in high-demand markets.

A Step-By-Step Guide on How to Sell Leads

Here is a detailed plan to help you start winning leads.

- Start by organizing your lead offering. Establish what your products will be by selecting one or more lead verticals. Having done this, you have to decide what your lead offering will be; this means deciding if they will be sold in packages or if you wish to invoice your clients on each purchase they make. When you sell leads exclusively, you sell to one buyer per lead, while selling nonexclusively means you sell to multiple buyers per lead. You could choose to do both.

- Build a buyer network. Having established your lead offering and how to acquire leads, you need to get together a network of buyers to buy your leads. For instance, brands need to push their products to specific target markets. You have to dedicate efforts to finding and working with your lead buyers.

- Establish lead distribution logic. Effective lead distribution is a crucial component of a company's income. Select the kind of lead distribution logic you wish to utilize. This gives you options that allow brands to maximize their profits.

- Build lead purchasing options. How do clients receive leads purchased from your brand? You have to build up options on how to go about that. You could either send it to the buyer's email, post it on their CRM, or post it on the client's portal to enable them to access it at their leisure. You also have to specify how you charge your clients if they want to purchase leads from your brand.

Hosting Workshops and Tutorials

Hosting workshops and tutorials is an easy way to monetize your social media. The topic can be any topic ranging from photography, language, technology, marketing, etc.

This is another form of selling your course, just that this time around, it'll be captured in a video. You'll make a video of yourself teaching the subject matter while your audience watches or downloads it. Online tutorials could be hosted on platforms like Zoom. You have the option of creating a website where you would host this tutorial.

Online tutorials are very beneficial because they can offer you a passive income stream. You can make a tutorial once and then sell it over and over again. Humans in their quest for more knowledge—in areas they have little knowledge in—will keep buying and buying. You can deliver to students from different time zones all over the world with no additional effort. It is like creating a system that pays you consistently over time.

All you have to do is organize the website in such a way that you can only get access to the materials if you pay for the class. Another way to go about it is by giving a small sample from the tutorial for free and directing them to your pay offerings where they can gain wider knowledge in that field. This works most of the time.

There are also websites like Udemy and Skillshare, Teachable, and Ruzuku where you can market your courses online.

Pricing can be an issue when you try to balance between making your profit and making the course affordable for students. To help in your decision, you could check similar courses to see how they go about their pricing, then fix yours.

Challenges of Monetizing Your Social Media

Just like every other phenomenon in life, there are challenges to monetizing social media. These include a list of hurdles a person or influencer has to go through while trying to make the most out of social media. It is not always easy to move an audience from social media space to buying products from you, no matter the tactics you employ. It takes patience, perseverance, and commitment for you to start seeing results. And when you do, it takes skills and even more money to maintain the level you are at.

1. **Conflicted goals**: To sell on social media platforms means to drop a percentage of your profit to these platforms. To promote your businesses on social media, you have to pay for ads. And with the price for ads plummeting year in and year out, it is becoming a challenge. This is a challenge to businesses on social media who are conflicted between trying to make a profit for themselves and making their products affordable for all.

2. **Monetization of user information**: Social media monetization poses a challenge to social media users who make use of the platform for relaxation and to blow off steam. By simply liking, swiping, clicking, and scrolling on social media spaces, your information is decoded and channeled down to monetary purposes, and next you are bombarded with advertisements about posts you liked. This makes social media a complete marketplace, which is a downside for its other purposes.

3. **Manipulation of algorithms**: In a bid to promote big businesses who paid for sponsored ads, advertisements, etc., the social media platform tries to demote the algorithms of small businesses, leading to low sales for them. Product searches get manipulated by ecommerce platforms to favor paid sellers.

4. **Restrictions on brands**: Social media platforms place restrictions on influencers monetizing their content on their platforms. Creators have to fulfill certain criteria before they can monetize on YouTube. They need to get up to 4,000 watch

hours in the previous 12 months, and that is not all. They also have to get over 1,000 subscribers on their channel before they start getting paid. Kuaishou initiated a program—Kuai Xiang—which requires creators/users to reach 10,000 followers before they incorporate advertisement features for creators to generate. These actions leverage the network of these content creators.

5. **Originality becomes lost**: In a bid to meet the requirements for content to acquire monetization, originality gets lost. There is nothing new on social media platforms anymore; only renewed, beautified, and edited versions of old content.

Tips for Monetizing Your Social Media

In this chapter, we have seen that one can make money through social media, as it is the new big thing in the world. Social media has gone beyond a platform for greeting old friends, stalking your crush, keeping in touch with families, posting pictures, and laughing at memes to a place where you can make massive money and grow businesses. Also, we have exhaustively examined mediums through which one can make money through social media and strategies to go about it. In this subsection, we are going to look at a few tips for monetizing your social media. You might have gotten a few ideas from this chapter, and I bet your heads are filled with a few ideas, but we're here to give you even more to add to your plates.

In the next chapter, we'll discuss the importance of social media collaborations and how you can utilize this opportunity to grow your brand.

Checklist

Attract the right audience. You have seen this a lot during the course of this book, and so you ask yourself, "How exactly do I go about attracting the right audience?"

Engage your audience. How do you do that? Publish polls to spark conversations with your audience. Also, ask questions for more in-depth dialogue. Here's an example: How old were you when you found out measles targets your memory cells? You could strike up conversations with your customers. Or you could ask questions that are close to your niche. By making conversations, you make your brand more memorable and help build trust, which will eventually lead to sales.

Sell directly from your social media pages: Instagram and Facebook have made online stores much easier. If you have an online store, Facebook has the Shop tab feature where you can create an online store. This feature lets you tag your products on both Facebook and Instagram.

Use chatbots: So long as you know your way around it, chatbots can be a powerful tool for monetizing your social media. They can be used to provide quick responses to the questions posed by customers.

Answer Frequently Asked Questions (FAQs): What are those questions that people always ask when it comes to your brand? You could answer these questions using creative methods like making content out of them; for instance, making videos, reels, etc. Some brands pin frequently asked questions to their highlights on their Instagram accounts for customers to easily access. You could do that as well.

Promote your mailing lists the same way you would promote your products as emails have proved to be one of the best ways to make sales.

Embrace testimonials: Testimonials are another way to build trust with your audience. This helps reassure customers when buying from you and encourages them to do business with you.

Chapter 7:

Navigating Collaborations

Human beings are an ultrasocial species—and our nervous systems expect to have others around us. –Emiliana Simon-Thomas, Ph.D.

They say no man is an island for a reason. It's not just because man is not dry land surrounded by water, because of course we are not, but because man needs association to survive. For thousands of years since the evolution of man, humans have thrived as a species through connection with one another. Right from when man hunted animals, gathered food, and settled in lands, we did it in groups, which shows how important it is for humans to be in touch with other humans.

In modern societies, the need for collaboration cannot be overemphasized. This is why companies have different sections to keep them running. The union of people with knowledge in different fields makes the company move. The knowledge from the guys in the IT department, marketing department, accounting departments, etc., ensure the smooth running of the business.

Collaboration cuts across every sphere of life, even in social media influencing. This chapter is going to explain what collaboration is, why it is important in social media influencing, its benefits, and how to go about it.

What Is Collaboration?

Collaboration simply means working with people from other teams or departments to accomplish a shared goal. Merriam-Webster dictionary defines "collaboration" as working jointly with others or together, especially in an intellectual endeavor.

Collaboration has to do with teamwork void of hierarchy; everyone working together and bringing in their input for the betterment of the group as a whole. Social media collaboration means when joining forces with another brand or other social media influencers. Why is collaboration important, especially among influencers?

Importance of Collaboration

The right social media influencers are people who fit your business demographic and have influence over people who are considered to be in your target market. It is only reasonable for a brand to collaborate with this set of people to further expand their businesses to a wider reach.

There are so many benefits that come with collaboration. Here are a few reasons why you should try collaborating with social media influencers for the smooth running of your business:

- It increases brand awareness.

- It builds trust and loyalty between customers and the brand.

- It helps in strengthening a customer's satisfaction.

- It helps to increase brand engagement.

- It helps increase conversion rates.

- It boosts the confidence customers have in a brand.

- It expands the brand's reach.

- It confirms the brand's originality.

- Brands get to create a connection with a wider audience/market.

These and more are the importance of collaborating with an influencer who has significant influence over a brand's target market. We didn't go into detail because some of these points have been discussed previously in other chapters.

How to Approach and Plan Collaboration

Having seen the importance of collaboration to your brand, what can brand owners do to approach and plan a successful collaboration?

What Is the Value of Your Audience?

It is very important to understand the value of your audience: What input do they add to your brand? Understanding the value of your audience goes a long way in understanding how to plan collaboration.

Set Your Goals

Before going into collaboration, brands have to ask themselves what goal this collaboration should meet. The goals have to be quantifiable, as this will enable the brand to understand whether the collaboration was a success or if it was a complete waste of time. Where the engagements or reach does not convert to sales, the point of the collaboration becomes useless. An increase in the number of sales does not equate to success; it is only successful when there are massive sales and returns. So, that should be the way to quantify your goals: the number of sales you should get and the number of returning customers. Wider reach or increase in followers should all be secondary. While listing out your goals, you have to brainstorm what social media platform will be your focal point.

Your Brand Should Be Consistent

While planning a collaboration, you have to ensure that your brand is consistent. To ascertain this, you have to list your priorities and ensure that the values of the influencer you want to hire align with the values of your brand. You also have to confirm if your products complement those of the other party. Finally, you have to ensure that the audience of your potential partner makes sense for your brand.

Find Collaborators Who Aren't Competitors

While collaboration is important, be sure not to do so with your competitors. Since you share a target audience with them, it would be counterproductive to confuse potential customers about which brand to choose. The more prudent option is to partner with brands that are in a different niche, so that you can share a symbiotic relationship with them.

Define Roles and Responsibilities

Setting up your goals and expectations from the collaboration is one step toward the success of the said collaboration. This is because in doing that, you assign roles and responsibilities to different team members or each person, holding them accountable for their compliance and noncompliance. While setting out the goals, you have to determine if the collaboration is a long-term partnership or short-term; for instance, during the period of a promotion. Some of the things that should be planned include: who has the responsibility of creating content; who responds to customers' questions; who has the responsibility of distribution of revenue; and what pages will the audience be led to.

Do Not Compromise the Trust of Your Audience

You have to protect the reputation of your brand by selling authentic and not substandard products. Trust is very fragile and can easily be broken, and it would be injurious to your reputation and brand name if it is soiled with mistrust as a result of inferior products. Compromising the trust of your audience not only puts your brand at risk of public criticism but also ruins the reputation of the hired influencer.

Benefits from the Collaboration Should Serve Both Parties

As a brand, you should bear in mind that the collaboration should not only enrich you and leave the other party out to dry. The collaboration should serve both parties. What does the other brand or influencer coming into collaboration with you stand to gain from the partnership? One way to determine this is by promoting each other on your social media posts. Promoting your influencer helps increase the reach of your paid posts, and it also shows appreciation to the influencer for creating content for your brand.

Use the Right Tools

You need the right tools to have a successful conversation with each other (brand and influencer). This would help foster the relationship between the brand and the social media influencer. Make use of social media management and content tools to assist in building and managing posts and content creation.

- Content creation tools like Canva Pro allow members to create content. Media management tools like Hootsuite allows many people to access and manage social media from one place.

- Setting up analytics will help measure how well your campaigns are working and show how to make changes where necessary.

Create a Story Guide

Humans relate to stories. This is because everyone has a story, and their story makes them who they are. What is the story behind the establishment of the brand? How can you make it appealing to your audience so that they will buy into it? If you do not make use of stories, you could create a theme for the collaboration. Choose a movement that would appeal to people's emotions and get them talking. It could be a charitable cause, something that gives back to society. A bank could make a collaboration with a fashion brand, and the theme here would be fashion. A good example is a collaboration between Spotify and Starbucks.

Align Your Collaboration With Seasonal Events

During periods such as Christmas, Easter, Thanksgiving, etc., businesses tend to get a lot of traffic online. Brands could cue in collaboration during festive periods to boost sales.

Also, at the beginning of seasons like the first day of summer, back to school, etc., brands could cue in collaboration to increase sales, but make sure your brand fits into the season. For instance, a tech company has no business with the first day of summer sales; instead, brands on the fitness stream would cash out big time during this period. This is because demand for swimming trunks and suits will be on the rise, for example.

Ways to Collaborate on Social Media

Influencer Gifting

This is when a brand gives a gift of their product to an influencer with no strings attached. By *with no strings attached,* we mean that the brand does not expect a review from or charge the influencer. This is one of the cheapest ways to buy into the heart of an influencer and foster long-term relationships with them. This would also show which influencer genuinely loves your product. They will write a review and post on their social media if they genuinely loved your product. This is also a form of proving the authenticity of your product, since the audience sees that the influencer is not getting paid to post the brand's product and it's coming out of the influencer's love for this product. This could foster collaboration between the influencer and the brand as time goes on.

- Seek influencers who would most likely love and be genuinely interested in your products. Ensure that the influencer's demographic would be interested in your product. You could make use of Modash to find creators who are in the same niche as your brand. Modash is an influencer discovery tool that you could also use to determine if their followers would benefit your brand. You can monitor the influencer's followers, engagements, etc.

- Customize your brand products.

- Offer a partnership, affiliate link, or commission where the post is successful.

- Seek the influencer's permission before reposting their posts, just like in reposting UGCs.

- Make use of Modash to measure the success of your influencer gifting and see if it has a positive yield. Modash will track the engagements on the post.

Sponsored Posts

We see sponsored posts every day—we visit our Instagram pages, and we see posts made by influencers with tags like "paid partnership with…" just beneath their usernames. In sponsored posts, influencers post a brand's product in exchange for a fee, unlike gifts where they do not have to pay. Most brands use these sponsored posts to test if they can go into collaboration with a social media influencer.

You can make the most out of sponsored posts as a brand by contacting different influencers in your field. As we said before, people are moved by what they see. The more they see relevant influencers posting your product at all times, the more it increases their likelihood of buying such products, especially where these influencers are trusted and have good relationships with their audience.

Also, give your influencers a rundown of your expectations from a sponsored post. This goes a long way in making them work in that direction, which will help the brand reach its goal faster.

Some influencers have fake followers, which is why we said previously that a huge number of followers does not determine influence; rather, it is the number of engagements an influencer gets that determines their influence. Brands going into partnership with these influencers should take note of this. They should be able to audit accounts with fake followings using tools designed to do so. Sites that offer influencer and follower audits include:

- Pathsocial

- inBeat

- HypeAuditor

- Grin

Monitor your influencer's campaign market to see which influencer gives you the maximum return on investments (ROI).

Giveaways

Everyone loves giveaways, and everyone looks forward to a giveaway, especially from a brand that they fancy. Business owners take advantage of this to draw traffic to their businesses. An influencer could make use of traffic to gather quality leads for the brand which hired them. They come up with different ideas on how to go about it.

For instance, the influencer gives instructions on how to enter a contest to win a product. They may ask a question, most probably about the product, then determine the winner from who gives the best answer and has the most likes to their replies. The winner gets a product from the brand for free, and this would motivate them. This would help drag traffic to the post and the brand alike. The more people like the product, the more likely the success of the partnership.

There is also an option for co-branded giveaways where brands with similar audiences join forces to conduct a giveaway for their brand. Each brand uses its influence to get even more audience with the giveaway. Although one person or a minimum number of people wins the giveaway, the amount of traffic gathered during that period would lead to eventual sales.

The essence of giveaways is to boost conversation and request customer actions. Get people talking about your brand.

To go about the sales, the influencer should go through some steps like the following:

- The influencer must explain the rules of the giveaway clearly for people to understand.

- The product used for the giveaway must be enticing enough for people to participate.

- The brand has to get the permission of participants before making use of their user-generated content.

Brand Ambassador Programs

When you think about a brand, there is usually a face that comes to your mind. These people are not the owners, nor are they executives of the brand. These people are called brand ambassadors.

Brand ambassadors are influencers who are long-term partners of a brand. They are paid to promote your business at all times. They usually have a fixed term for their contract; it could be a year, two, or whatever period is specified in the terms of the contract. The brand pays the influencer, who in turn creates content for it and brings traffic to the brand's website. A brand ambassador is like the face of your brand; therefore, they embody the values of your brand. They're loyal, committed, and original to your brand, therefore they will not partner with your competitor.

Not just anyone can be your brand ambassador, so you have to choose only trusted influencers who genuinely love your brand/product. Make their membership exclusive, since not just anyone can become a brand ambassador.

The Job of Brand Ambassadors

- They act as the face of the brand.

- They have the job of promoting the brand on a myriad of social media platforms.

- They are experts and must have in-depth knowledge of the brand.

- They are not only limited to social media; they get involved in product marketing, launches, and event planning.

- The primary goal of any brand ambassador is to increase brand awareness.

- They communicate with consumers for feedback and give out recommendations.

Characteristics a Brand Ambassador Must Possess

- They must be professional.

- They have to be equal to the task given to them.

- They must know about marketing and how to go about it to support the brand they are representing.

- They must have passion for the job assigned to them, and they must love the brand; that way, representing the brand flows naturally.

- They must be trustworthy. No one wants to employ a dishonest person as a brand ambassador.

- They must be active online. They need to have established influence over a significant amount of people, as well as a larger following on social media platforms.

Account Takeovers

Most times, the person behind the periodic posting on a brand profile/account is not the owner of the brand. They employ influencers who have good copywriting skills and knowledge about managing a business profile to maximize profit and increase visibility.

An account takeover is a person who takes over the account of a brand to post, create, and share content on behalf of the brand. This is a fantastic way through which brands and influencers collaborate and promote content. It is a win-win situation whereby the brand brings in someone who will bring value to their followers, and the person reaches a new audience with their content.

How to Organize Social Media Account Takeovers

- Set your goals. These goals will influence the strategy for the takeover. Some goals could be increasing brand awareness, engaging the community, and promoting a product. Decide how long the takeover will take and what kind of content will be promoted during the takeover.

- Choose your guest. Anyone can work as your account takeover. It could be a worker, an influencer, or a customer. However, influencers are the most common guests for takeovers.

- Choose the type of takeover. It could be done with a Facebook post, Instagram stories, or by going live on YouTube.

- Execute the takeover. There are two ways to go about a social media takeover: a semi-account takeover and a full-account takeover. Where there is a full-account takeover, the guest has access to the company's account; however, where there is a partial takeover, the guest sends whatever they want to post through mail to the company to be posted on their behalf.

- Wrap up. After the takeover has come to an end, evaluate the performance during and after the process. How many followers did you gain? How engaged was your brand?

Content Collaborations

Ever handled the job of creating content for your brand alone? No matter how good you are, you are bound to tire out, and this is where you will need the contribution of others. Some days we just run out of ideas and fresh content, and we begin to question ourselves. There should be room for another person, especially one who is grounded in that field to help us out.

Now, you may ask, what is content collaboration? Why is it important to my brand? This section will answer your questions and more. When you think about content collaboration, what comes to mind are group projects from high school. You get paired up with your classmates who end up dumping the whole workload on you alone. It sucks, but I assure you, that is far from what content collaboration is.

Content collaboration simply means coming together with people for the sole purpose of creating content. It could be a series of content or a large content project. In content collaboration, you bring in diverse people with skills who are willing to put in the effort to make your projects a success. Content collaborators should also be willing to commit, which is why a brand owner has to be careful when choosing them.

Product Collaborations

This is all about setting up a team with other brands to create new products or improve an already existing one. Product collaboration serves the audience of both brands and forms what seems like a partnership. The two brands leverage their reputations and create a product they could not have created alone. Since they both have already established audiences, they both share gains from their audiences.

- Since launching a product together with another brand involves high stakes and is a huge step for your brand, you could get the help of very popular influencers who you trust will achieve a positive return on investments.

- These influencers should have the lead in creating the new collection. This is because they know what to do and how to handle the job better.

- A better way is to hire an influencer with whom you have partnered in the past and received good results from the partnership. This is because you share a relationship with them, and you trust their capabilities.

- Tease the potential product collaboration by leaking information about it online through posts and blogs. Encourage your influencer to do the same, with statements like, "Do you know the next big thing?" This is to create anticipation among customers for what is coming next.

- Include all of your strategies and manufacturing details in the influencer contract. This is to avoid misunderstanding in the future and to make the influencer aware of what is at stake.

Some examples of product collaborations over the years include the following:

- **Nokia and Microsoft**. Both have similar audiences, which are in the tech area. The two brands in 2019 announced their collaboration. Nokia, being a networking powerhouse, combined with Microsoft's expansive cloud computing to help communication providers create high-end solutions like smart cities, etc. Their partnership would foster the business to new levels of connectivity and automation.

  They aimed at making life better for their customers alike by making use of their strengths to lengthen the lifetime of their customers. Although their first collaboration in 2011 wasn't a success, they came together again in 2019 to form an even stronger bond than the first.

- **HubSpot and Freshbooks**. Their partnership was aimed at the same customers; however, they were at different levels in the workflow. HubSpot is a sales software brand, and FreshBooks is an accounting software. After their collaboration, they took different roles in maximizing and satisfying the needs of their audience. While HubSpot took over the role of optimizing the market, FreshBooks had the role of managing invoices and receiving payments online.

Hosting Events

Sometimes a way to create engagement or awareness for your brand goes beyond social media, physical contact, or experience with people. Here, people come face-to-face with the people behind their gigantic screens and engage with them one on one. One way to go about this is by hosting or organizing events.

Hosting events for your brand is like a magnet for influencers to have an experience of what your brand is like. It has also proved to stimulate the brand's exposure. To promote their products and services, brands organize and host events. They also focus on strengthening their relationship with their audience.

What Are the Benefits of Hosting Events?

Brands stand the chance to gain a lot of benefits by hosting events, and they include the following:

- **Brand awareness**: Through hosting events, the company links up with other companies with great reputations. This would in turn generate awareness for the brand.

- **Engagement**. People are always looking forward to exciting experiences, even if it entails learning a new product or closing a deal—where the event fosters this, it could lead to engagements.

- **Leads**. Events are a great opportunity to generate leads, and this is a result of the personal information submitted by participants on the registration for the events. Information like emails given by the participants can generate leads such that the brands make use of email marketing strategies to approach these leads.

- **Sales**. Sometimes it doesn't happen immediately, but when it doesn't happen immediately, it doesn't mean that the event was a failure.

- **Link up with influencers**. Events attract influencers, and if you go about your promotion the right way, it will attract the right number and quality of influencers. Gracing your event gives you an opportunity to link up with them.

Forms of Hosting Events

- trade shows

- conferences

- networking events

- product launch

- virtual events

- workshops

How to Plan and Host an Event

1. Set up a goal. Here, you define your business objectives so you can strategize the event to pursue that course and measure your success at the end of the day.

2. Set out a budget. How much money is the brand's pocket going to cough up to host the event? The money should be such that

it does not affect the income of the brand, bearing in mind what is available to the company.

3. Set up staff. These people will be in charge of planning and managing the event. They are professionals from different departments in your company—the IT department, the sales department, marketing, and event producers.

4. Set event schedule. A schedule should be set up for how the event will progress. This serves as a guide for how the staff will go about planning the event.

5. Set up a venue. Where would be most appropriate to host your event? A hired hall or somewhere within the company's vicinity? The type of event you're hosting determines the venue to be used.

6. Promote the event. Now, you will need people to grace your event, and the only way you can get people at your event is by promoting it. Make use of social media platforms, and other media platforms like television and radio, to announce the date of the event. How far and how well the promotion goes will determine the eventual turnout.

Guest Blogging

A great way to achieve content collaboration is to have influencers talk about your brand on their podcast, website, or social media pages.

Sometimes you have an idea, but you do not know how to go about it. If this is your situation, content collaboration is what you should be thinking about. Your job is to look for influencers who are ready to accept pitches to pitch your idea and create great content out of it. You will then pay them at the end of the project.

1. Find influencers who have podcasts, blogs, or websites with high domain ratings. Make sure they also fall under your niche.

2. Reach out to them and find out if they accept guest blog posts on their pages.

3. Pitch ideas they would be interested in.

4. Create informative, well-written, and engaging blog posts they can post on their websites.

5. If you are not great with content writing, you could assign the job to someone who can do it well.

6. Attach your link to the blog post in a way that doesn't appear spammy or overly promotional.

Tips on Building and Maintaining Relationships With Influencers and Brands

Influencers are not just marketing tools, they are humans with feelings and problems, so it is important to treat them as such. Maintaining a relationship with them goes a long way in showing them how important they are to your brand. There are so many benefits that come with building and maintaining relationships with influencers. It fosters growth, stability, trust, and so many other virtues.

A good way to achieve this is by sending personalized emails to influencers like you would do for a collaborator. This will help bond the relationship between the influencer and the brand and also yield positive results.

The life of an influencer involves getting dozens of messages to their emails, socials, etc. Sometimes messages get so bulky and they leave so many unread that your brand's message could be one of those messages they overlook. A good way to call the attention of influencers is by seeking creative ways to reach out to them, those that they would not be able to ignore. For instance, host an event that will drag them to the venue where you can reach out to them one-on-one.

Long-term relationships help build a kind of bond and trust between influencers and the brand. There is loyalty and mutual respect between the two compared to one-off collaborations. The influencer grows with the brand and shares an intimacy and strong bond with the brand that feels like family. Again, most influencers will welcome long-term relationships compared to one-offs.

Imagine that after getting a job done, your payment is not commensurate with the effort you put in to get the job done. You would be bitter and hold resentment for whoever paid you that way. Now, think about influencers who do not get paid appropriately for the job they do for a brand. It is not only unfair, but it will also create a bad relationship between the influencer and the brand, and they will not look forward to working with that brand in the future. It is only fair that influencers get paid appropriately. To foster a long-lasting relationship between brand and influencer, brands should do what is right.

For any relationship to thrive, communication is important. The difference between best friends and those in bad relationships is communication. How often do you communicate with your influencers? And in what manner do you communicate with them? Brands should maintain good relations with their influencers by updating them on the happenings in the company and not only reaching out to them on campaign-related topics. Imagine the only reason a person reaches out to you is when they need you, and nothing else. What kind of relationship would you have with such a person? This is why in everything, communication is important. You could send them congratulatory messages on their wins, send a thank you message after a collaboration, or send personalized emails to them wishing them happy birthday and commenting on their posts. This would show how much the brand cares about its personal journey and desire to create bonds.

Inviting influencers to brand events such as workshops, product launches, conferences, trade shows, etc., hints at how important those influencers are to your brand, your interest in them, and your intention to share your experience with them to create a mutual relationship. All the while, the brand should be sending messages through emails and posts. Personal contact fosters a bonded relationship, and influencer-brand relationships are no exception.

How well do you, as a brand, know your influencers? A brand-influencer relationship does not have to be rigid and hierarchical just because it is professional. You could know your influencers and yet be professional about it. Brands must know their influencers and understand their audience. This way, they can connect with them on a deeper level, making them comfortable with the brand. In the future, when they are presented with another deal, they will most likely work with you again.

From time to time, you should give gifts to your influencers. Gifts could be a product from the brand or anything else. This makes the influencers feel loved and special and have a sense of exclusivity. These gifts are different from the formal payments that should be given to the influencers. Seek creative ways to gift them. It could be during seasonal holidays like Christmas, Thanksgiving, Easter, etc., or their birthdays. Periodic gifting has proven to form bonds between influencers and brands and will make the influencer do even better with their jobs.

Helping influencers to grow should be part of the goals a brand has for its influencers. Although brands hire them to improve their digital presence, create brand awareness, and maximize sales, an influencer-brand relationship should be beneficial to both parties. So long as the growth of the influencer is positive and does not clash with the personal interest of the brand, it should be allowed. Brands should also include their quotas to ensure their influencers grow.

To succeed at any venture, it's important that you learn about the experiences of those who have walked that path before you. In the next chapter, we'll do exactly that.

Checklist

	Treat influencers as collaborators.
	Reach out to influencers in creative ways.
	Prioritize long-term relationships.
	Offer fair compensation.

	Maintain open communication.
	Invite influencers to events.
	Know your influencers.
	Offer hospitality.
	Offer support to influencers.

Chapter 8:

Lessons Learned From Seasoned

Social Media Influencers

There is a Belgian proverb that says that experience is the comb that nature gives to us after we have become bald. The truth of this proverb comes to the fore in everything that we do as human beings. After accumulating hundreds of thousands of minutes performing our various tasks and going about our various lives, we gain what we call experience; an accumulation of everything that we have learned about how to do things in more efficient ways over time. Experience is something that can only be gained over time, and it changes your views and perspectives about certain things.

Experience cannot be taught, which is why the words of older people are often taken with much consideration. In the social media influencing world, you are still a newbie and will soon come to find that taking the advice of older and more experienced social media influencers could be of enormous benefit to you.

Qualities of a Great Influencer

To some, influencing is an art form through which they find happiness. To others, it is a means to an end. There is no compulsory meaning to social media influencing, and there is a place for everyone. Influencers could be many things, and each influencer is different. As each influencer is different from the next, the things that may set one influencer apart from another may be a lot. However, upon studying seasoned influencers, there are some general qualities that exist in nearly every great social media influencer. Some of these include the following.

Dedication

Dedication refers to being committed or zealous about something. Dedication is such an important quality as an influencer that it is often the difference between a successful person and an unsuccessful person. In the world of influencing, there is constantly a lot going on, and it can often be quite suffocating—it becomes easy to simply give up and stop striving to be better. However, even in traditional work settings, it is pleasing to employers when an employee shows dedication and commitment to their role by doing things such as devoting extra time to work, improving their skills and competencies to become better, and other similar acts. Showing dedication helps you develop as a professional and aids your development as a person as well.

An influencer with dedication will possess an intense drive to do better and produce more favorable results in their career. Their goals and strategies are aligned, and they are ready to put in the extra work needed to become better. With such a great quality being displayed, their commitment often does not end at benefitting just them. It is very common to see company-wide changes when one person begins to show dedication and passion for the job. Their demeanor begins to affect everyone around them, and their coworkers often begin to put in just as much effort so that they may be recognized as well.

In the same vein, an influencer showing passion and dedication in their work will directly or indirectly influence other influencers and social media users to develop a hunger and drive for success and progress. There are many advantages to showing dedication as a social media influencer. Some include the following:

- **You gain access to even more opportunities**: Dedication as a trait is something that can be spotted a mile away. It is a highly sought trait in professionals that usually signifies that they are great to work with and will deliver great results. When you display dedication in your daily routines as an influencer, it spreads beyond simply just being something that you do. It begins to permeate and show in your appearance, how you address your audience, and so on.

Companies, brands, and other influencers are constantly on the lookout for new ways to take their products to the next level. For this to happen, they often need to work with others. In deciding who to work with from a large pool of people, regardless of talent and competence, a host of other factors often play into this decision. The moment that you choose to display dedication, you will stand out and be considered for more opportunities by others. People who have already worked with you will spread the word about your dedication, and what's more, people will want to associate their brands with someone with such a desirable quality.

- **You will develop yourself further**: Stagnating in one's career becomes easy when a person lacks dedication. They lack the commitment and drive to constantly develop new skills and goals that will make them become better at what they do. Dedication gives you the drive to constantly give more to your work. This will likely include using your off hours to research how to be better and learn better techniques. It also involves plenty of practice and hard work. However, as someone with dedication, the constant will to become better makes all of these easier to develop.

As you constantly train and better yourself, you will start to develop skills that even translate outside of your chosen career path. Your dedication will bring a desire to learn, which will inevitably come along with skills outside of what you are already good at.

- **You become an inspiration to others**: With the dedication and commitment of a professional, you will inevitably inspire more people to want to be like you. Dedication is an enviable trait, and luckily, it is learnable as well. When people around you see your commitment either directly from you or indirectly through the work that you put into your craft as an influencer, it tends to make them feel inclined to become more like you in that manner.

Showing dedication will inspire others to follow after the positive traits that you have shown. There are a couple of advantages that come from showing dedication as an influencer. Some include the following:

- **Exceptional work output**: When you are dedicated to something, it is often pretty hard to hide it—dedication usually shines forth and can often be quite obvious since it is such a desirable human trait. As something that you are committed to, you will often care more about your career than the average influencer. This means that you will put more into your work than normal, and this will result in your output and productivity exceeding regular levels.

- **Top quality work**: Those who are dedicated to their jobs are more likely to produce high-quality work than other people. They become more involved and critical about the various details of their work and inspect their work every step of the way before it makes its way to their clients. Possessing dedication as an influencer will naturally translate to you producing higher quality work, since you are deeply invested in its success, and this means that you will produce the highest quality work that you are able to.

- **Your attitude changes**: Being dedicated can positively affect your personal feelings about the subject of your dedication. For example, if an employee was dedicated to their work, they would be more willing to start work every day, they would be more willing to help out when needed, and they would be more enthusiastic about spotting opportunities to be more useful at work. Dedicated employees also motivate their colleagues to be better as people and as coworkers.

Passion

Passion is an emotion that often shows up in people when they care deeply about something. It shows up in the different things that we do when we are passionate about them. This is why it is important for influencers and social media enthusiasts in general to make content about the things that they like or are interested in, as a lack of passion will later betray their pursuits.

When you pursue content that people will like and set as your main focus, you might end up doing something that you are uninterested in yourself, and this will lead to a lack of passion and enthusiasm when working. If passion were present, you would be more likely to ask questions, follow along, learn quickly, and share stories about your passion.

When watching the content of influencers with passion for their content and career, there is a different kind of enthusiasm, creativity, and originality to their work. The passion is often very visible in their actions and how they carry themselves. It is essential to have passion because viewers and your consumers can sense a lack of passion, and this will lead to a loss of potential and current followers. This is why some content influencers refuse to make videos or content when they are not feeling like themselves. A lack of passion is not a good thing to show to an audience, as this can often make them feel undervalued and underappreciated, resulting in a loss of their patronage.

Being passionate about your work can influence your lifestyle and choices in more ways than one. When you have passion for what you do, it tends to affect you in a few of the following ways:

- **You develop confidence**: In today's societies, people are often forced by their parents or guardians to do things that they do not want to do a lot of the time. This could be anything from studying something that does not align with their passions, being forced to relocate to other countries, or cutting off friendships with other people. As a result of that, there are millions of people today doing things that they would otherwise not be doing and have no interest in. A lack of passion abounds across the world today, and this is highly detrimental to both mental and physical health. When you possess a passion for something that you are involved in, you become more involved, more aware, and more confident. You are more willing to acknowledge your weaknesses and develop your strengths, which often blossoms into even more confidence.

- **You leave your comfort zone**: Passion can take a man so far that he does not realize that he has left home. Having a passion for your social media career will often translate into you doing more than you are comfortable with. People are usually scared and hesitant to go ahead with new things and experiment, especially with things that they are not comfortable with or used to. Passion for something can make you more willing to experiment and discover new things—you begin to experiment on your own and try every idea possible because you are interested and involved.

Originality

Authenticity is a trait that is missing among many social media influencers today. There is a drive to be like the popular people on social media, and this often results in upcoming enthusiasts molding their entire personas around these popular identities. The result is a monotonous and bland social media space with many of the same types of content littered everywhere. It is rather tempting to abandon everything that makes you original and different to model yourself into what you think people will like.

This is such a big mistake that breaks careers before they even start, and it is a bad practice that should not be encouraged. If you are creating the same content in the same way as everyone else, there is no reason for anyone to stay with you when they could go to others and get the exact same things that you offer. When you display originality as a social media influencer, people fall in love with who you are and not just the persona that you show them.

It is much like interviewing for a job and pretending to have all the certifications and requirements that the job requests. You are aware of what they want and falsify yourself to be considered by them. Even in this hypothetical scenario, this will only work short-term, because there will be some things that they require that you cannot fake—and the inevitable result is that you are exposed for being a fraud. In your quest to be a superstar social media influencer, it is best to embrace your originality, be authentic, and be yourself.

A lot of people today have grown up wearing masks. They have been told what to do and wear, as well as how to behave in order to not stand out. Standing out and being different is popular on social media, but the reality is different. You should not need to wear a mask around your audience. As a matter of fact, your audience needs to accept you for yourself. Your audience should be a space where you belong, not where you try to fit in and perform in order to impress people.

Being original means that you are true to yourself, your desires, and your goals. It means that you are real with yourself, admit your mistakes or faults, and accept them. When you are authentic, your values and goals automatically align with your original personality. You begin to exude contentment, passion, and authenticity. This is a good thing to have as a social media influencer, and it will eventually open you up to more opportunities and allow you access to a more loyal and loving fan base that identifies with you and accepts you for who you are.

Tips to Becoming a Better Influencer

For you to be a great influencer, you must first be a good influencer. To be counted worthy among the many different influencers in the world, you must perfectly understand your strengths as well as your weaknesses, and you must develop them in such a way that they cover for each other and flow seamlessly together. You will need to identify and grow in all aspects of your social media influence to be able to become even better. As an influencer, you will need to make sure that your voice is not merely screaming into the void with no one to listen.

Seasoned social media influencers are able to exude control over so much of their careers that they are able to make things happen at will. They are able to create trends on a whim, are able to get their audience to do whatever they want, and are able to control things that translate to a real-world influence. They are experts in taking ideas, selling those ideas to an audience, letting the audience know exactly what they want, and can direct attention wherever they please.

There are a couple of things you could work on to become an even better influencer than you already are. They include the following:

Practice and Train Persuasion

Persuasion is by itself such a wonderful skill. When persuasion is combined with other skills that a great social media influencer possesses, the result is a superstar influencer with the ability to command people to do almost anything that they ask. The best influencers understand that persuasion is not as simple as making people do what they want. Persuasion is a language—it is the art of meeting people at a common ground. Persuasion involves understanding what other people's pain points are, empathizing with them, and finally coming to a solution that benefits you or is in tandem with your goals.

You must show genuine consideration for their plights in order to establish your sincerity. You may then introduce a common interest in order to show the audience that you are also affected, and then you must relate with them emotionally, as this is important in order to persuade. After all of this is done, you may then use compelling words and actions to shift the dynamic to where you would like it to go. Persuasion is a skill that will be useful to you in all stages of your development as an influencer.

Develop Your Communication Skills

A social media influencer who cannot communicate properly with their audience is a social media influencer who is going to have a very hard time making it in the influencing space. As a social media influencer, communication exists in every facet of the trade. You are constantly communicating with your audience, brands, and with the viewers and readers of your content. Without communicating, it is impossible to influence anyone. Influencing in itself is a form of communication, so developing communication skills will develop your influence at the same time.

In order to possess influence, you must be able to easily communicate, direct, and share your thoughts with your chosen audience. Being able to successfully communicate, present, and share your content in an easily digestible way is the first step toward being able to influence your audience on social media. If you are not able to successfully communicate or share your thoughts with one person physically, the chances are that you will not be able to share them with thousands or millions of people on the internet.

Communication is how well you are able to interact with other people as well as how you are able to break down a difficult concept and share it with an audience so that they understand and receive all of the information that you are trying to pass. Developing your communication will benefit you immensely, as it is one of the most powerful tools that an influencer could possess.

Build Your Confidence

In order to exude any kind of influence in today's world, a sense of confidence is necessary. Confidence is a quality that can shine through in everything that you do, even outside of influencing. It is the ability to show certainty about a subject matter. This could be oneself, their plans, or other people. Having confidence means that you will not be afraid to do what needs to be done in order to succeed at whatever your goals might be. When you are capable of something, you are often more confident about your abilities in doing such a thing. You will naturally develop confidence in the qualities and skills that you are capable of doing at high levels.

You should look at your goals, passion, and plans and identify your strengths so that you may improve on them. You should constantly be on the search for whatever you can do to improve your skills and competencies, as this will drive your confidence up, and this will show in your content and further enhance your image to your followers and audience.

Confidence is an attractive trait that can bring people together from far and wide like a magnet. It is a trait that many people study and would like to emulate, as well as love to be around. Having confidence in your work is definitely going to be good for you as well, and you will see a transient result in your personal life and daily activities as well.

Be Intentional

A lot of content on the internet today is being made mindlessly. People have been fed full with success stories of influencers that made it to the top with the kind of generic content that is largely prevalent today. A lot of influencers thrive on social media through fake identities and personas that they have created to lead people to believe that they have luxurious and rich lifestyles which people want to copy and emulate. The result of this is the same mindless content all across the internet.

As someone looking to be a great influencer, you should aim to recognize and stay away from those monotonous content types. They often become old quite fast, and people lose their interest in them in a short period of time. You should look to create content that lasts and is remembered as original and different from other people. You should be intentional about making content that is not just another social media page on the internet, but one that stands for something different and is original in its own way.

Being intentional about the kind of content that you create and put out to the public helps you to build trust with your audience because they will definitely feel and understand that your content is different from what they usually consume, and they will love and follow you for that reason.

Share Your Journey Publicly

As you grow and develop as an influencer, it is only natural that you will come to face a lot of challenges and hardships on your way. From finding the right platform to growing your audience, even if you follow this guide to the letter, you might still encounter a few things that may pose problems for you. It is important to document these various things that occur. Your progress, your process, and your failures on your way to becoming a good influencer should be documented. This will allow you to gain data that you could use to further improve and develop yourself.

While it is good to document all your experiences, it is even better to share them with your audience. Documenting and sharing your successes and failures will allow you to develop a strong bond with your community of followers. They will begin to grow with you in a sense, and they often appreciate it when social media personalities show that things are not always perfect. It humanizes you to your audience and allows them to relate to you in a different manner.

In this chapter, we spoke about all of the different things you are presently doing as an influencer that you could be doing better. We talked about all of the things that seasoned social media influencers recommend, and we talked about a lot of tips that could help you become an even better influencer. It has been a great run, and we are finally rounding off. Keep reading to learn more.

Checklist

	Be likable. People are more likely to want to work with you if you are a likable person. They will also be more likely to watch your content and become part of your audience.
	Be passionate about your work. Passion shines forth in your work as an influencer.
	Keep up to date with the latest trends and happenings in your niche. News flies around quite fast and can get out of date just as quickly.
	Engage your audience in a respectful way that shows that you care about them. People can tell when you really care about them or when you are faking it. Faking it will lose you valuable consumers.
	Be authentic and original. Having the same content as every other person will not get you far as an influencer.
	Post and share consistently. You should aim to post your content as often as possible when you are just starting out. This helps imprint you in people's minds.

	Be thoughtful and intentional with your content. You can solve problems or answer questions, or even just teach people things they never knew.
	Keep an eye on your competitors. Monitor their strengths and weaknesses and use that information to develop yourself.
	Monitor your own strengths and weaknesses as well, and work on them both. This will help you become better in the long run.
	Document and keep note of your journey to being an influencer. You might encounter tricky situations in the future, and it helps to have a reference board to use in dealing with problems.
	Market yourself properly. It is essential that you develop good marketing skills so that you can sell yourself as well as possible and take every opportunity that comes your way.
	Utilize data analytics to better understand your target markets and what you can do better to reach them.
	Remember to ask questions when you are confused.
	You can offer your services for little to no charge to help push your recognition.
	Collaborate with other influencers.
	Utilize digital marketing tricks and best practices.
	Ensure you are posting your content at the best possible times for maximum visibility.
	Work on your brand identity. Be known for something and work with similar figures in that direction.
	Do not flood your followers with content. Posting consistently

	does not mean you should pester people.
	Moderate your advertisements. People can get turned off by excessive advertisements, so learn to balance them with your content.
	Gain technical knowledge about your chosen social media platform and technology. Tech-savvy influencers are significantly more sought-after.
	Be creative with your content and branding. Use your imagination in every aspect of your work. This will help you stand out.
	Be consistent with your content and posting. Social media algorithms tend to favor more consistent content.
	Do not be afraid to mess around and try new things. This can be helpful when you are in a creative rut.
	Ask for feedback and use the feedback to improve yourself. You must be able to see your work from another person's perspective.
	Take courses and consistently skill up to improve yourself. You need to constantly polish yourself to be the best.
	Work on your confidence and people skills. Real-life skills often translate to social media and improvements can be very useful to your career.
	Set goals for your career and try to make them specific and time bound. Use that to track your progress and push yourself.
	Take it easy and do not put unnecessary pressure on yourself. Being a success as an influencer takes time.
	Read books, articles, and other news sources to stay on top of trends and keep an eye out for best practices.

Conclusion

We have come to the end of our journey through this book that has guided you through everything about social media, including establishing yourself on various social media platforms, how to grow a career on social media, how to become an influencer, as well as all the various steps you need to take to be safe while doing it. You may confidently pick up this book, and after you are done reading it, you can be sure that you are well equipped with everything that you will need to become a successful social media influencer.

To get the best use out of this book, you should use it like a guide to get familiar with everything about social media, how to thrive on it, and how to go about establishing a career as a social media influencer.

Influence is the capacity to change the growth, behavior, or thought process of a person or thing without the use of force. Social media influence is how a person is able to affect others and their decisions and behaviors. A person can exert degrees of influence, and the more influence a person has, the more they are able to affect other people's behaviors. As the world has developed, every day there are more social media influencers than the previous day. This only confirms what has been suspected—that social media influencing is a rapidly growing market that is predicted to become one of the top market economies in the world.

Lessons Learned so Far

There are many things that could stand in the way of a person becoming a social media influencer. An influencer could face troubles with finding their niche community, they could find it hard to gather an audience, they may have trouble with their media visibility, or they may simply lack the consistency to push through and become great social media personalities. They may also face less technical issues specific to their careers, such as the pressure of maintaining an image for the public or maintaining their brand's reputation. They may also face creativity blocks or cyberbullying.

There are many threats for those who choose to walk this path. Influencers often have to deal with threats including but not limited to having their identities stolen, having their work copied, and having their intellectual properties duplicated. They all face the rigors of breaking into a niche community of people. The road to becoming an influencer is not easy; however, the ones who tread it may read this book and stand tall above these fears with the knowledge to conquer them.

The world has changed immensely in the past decade, with the majority of the world becoming so dependent on the internet that it has become a sort of replacement for traditional information sources. Society has integrated and become used to technology in ways such that it is now exclusively used over more traditional methods.

Social media websites and applications gain more users every day, and the number of active devices increases with each passing day, too. With such a large number of people possessing internet-enabled devices, there is a lot of power to be harnessed in that sphere. The advantages of being able to control or influence the information that flows to such a large number of people cannot be exaggerated.

Social media influence may be gained as a result of many factors including but not limited to your accomplishments, your contributions on social media, and your social class. Influential people are able to command and persuade people to work with them toward a common goal or perspective, or they may get people to do specific things that they want. There are various advantages to possessing social media influence in the world today. A person with social media influence may develop strong connections with powerful people and world leaders solely based on their ability to influence the thoughts and actions of a number of people.

Being able to master social media influencing will open you up to several benefits, including improvement in product sales, being able to pioneer trends and thought patterns, being able to affect major decisions and outcomes across the world, and so on. Social media influence can even affect the outcomes of political events, such as elections and debates. There are several uses and advantages to having social media influence. In a world of over eight billion people, being able to influence any number of people is a laudable feat worthy of emulation.

The possibilities of having access to such power are only limited by human imagination. People, however, have recently begun to come to terms with the fact that the power of social media is very real and quite potent. Movements and entire cultures have been started, changed, and affected by social media and its influencers, and people have no problem shelling out premium sums of money to access or control this power in some way or another. Influencer marketing has become a gigantic market worth several billion dollars and comes with the added advantage of being able to tell people what to do—money and influence is an irresistible combination.

Social Media Niches

Socialization among human beings has been revolutionized. Connection with one another has been simplified, people are able to find and locate lost friends and family, they are able to communicate in ways that were not possible decades ago, and reaching people across unfathomable distances has never been easier. The world has changed, and social media is a great contributor to that change. With the ever-progressing developments in technology, social media influencers will be the ones leading the charge in the near future, and all indications show this is a great career choice for all who venture into it in these times.

To properly control and harness all of the power that you could possibly wield as a social media influencer, the importance of a niche cannot be overemphasized. It is not mandatory to have a niche, and there are a number of successful influencers without niches. However, to give you the best chances of becoming a great influencer, deciding on a niche will be more beneficial to your career in the long term. Finding a niche allows you to stand out. When you find a niche, you have found something that is unique and specific to you.

A niche is beneficial in many ways. It allows people to relate to you on a different level and convinces them to listen to you more, since they can identify more with your message and your content. People naturally follow the content and people in whom they are interested. From food to travel and lifestyle, people constantly gravitate toward the content niches that interest them and that they can relate to. Making niche content will allow you to promote yourself more effectively and sell yourself better, automatically giving you a stronger potential for success on social media.

When you understand what exactly you are doing and who exactly you are doing it for, the process of creation becomes so much easier, as you can now devise clearly defined structures and plans for how your content should look and feel. You are better able to adjust your content to fit what your ideal clients find appealing and interesting. This will naturally help you develop authenticity, improve your visibility and reach, and also increase your knowledge and expertise in the field.

Discovering your niche also lets you get rid of the excess competition. You are able to focus your energy and separate yourself from the noise. You are no longer in a space where everyone is doing the same thing. You become unique and special in a different way from those around you and your competition.

You gain clarity and can identify what is important and what is not. Doing this will also allow your self-confidence to grow by leaps and bounds. Choosing a niche to focus on means that you are better able to utilize your talents and skills in a way that will help you succeed. There is a much higher chance of you coming out on top, because your niche lets your talents and strengths develop and you know more about yourself and your weaknesses.

As a social media influencer, identifying your specialization is crucial since it establishes you as a professional in your sector. It enables you to grow a devoted and active fan base that is interested in what you have to say and how you say it, and can aid in the development of your brand into a powerful one. When talking about social media influencing, having a niche specialization makes it easier for brands and businesses to locate you. It also allows you to establish credibility and authority within your industry while assisting you in producing the best possible content that is both relevant and consistent for your audience.

A niche also allows you to make more money than you would potentially make without a niche. You are able to find the right customers, and they are more interested in purchasing your product because that is their niche, and they are willing consumers.

Social Media Influencing and Target Markets

After finding a niche, there is still more for you to do. You must find a niche and then you must find a target audience. Finding a niche usually solves this problem, as the niche that you choose often dictates who your target market is. However, sometimes this is not the case. Finding a target market as a social media influencer can be quite hard to do.

As an influencer, marketing on social media is quite an effective strategy for reaching your target demographic. The optimal method for you will be specific to your brand's unique characteristics. It will depend on the type of content that you offer, the type of products or services that you offer, as well as your specific niche.

There are several existing and new ways to identify your target market as an influencer. Prior to considering who would be interested in what you have to offer, you will need to first determine who your current consumers are. After finding them out, you need to find out which corner of the internet or social media they hang out in. The list is long; however, you may search for groups that appear to be a good fit for your potential clients and consumers on sites such as Facebook, Instagram, X, Pinterest, or even LinkedIn.

Finding your target audience is a great step in your journey toward becoming an effective and professional social media influencer. You would ideally want to use your posts and content to influence the target market that you have decided on. Target markets may generally come from places such as your family and friends, other clients and consumers of your niche content or specialty, and lastly, the general public that is unaware of your niche.

It is rather important that the social media content that you post matches the interests and sensibilities of the target audience you have chosen. For instance, as a fashion designer, you will need to share articles, videos, pictures, and other art forms on current trends and the latest styling advice in order to remain relevant to this audience. Influencers on social media are the ones who possess more sizable fan bases than the average person. They frequently have a significant impact on their audience and as we have come to see, can also sometimes be the impetus for societal changes. The allure of the profession as well as how easy it has become to start has encouraged an increase in the number of influencers.

As a result of their proven advantages, businesses around the world are also beginning to recognize the importance of social media and social media influencers. They are able to enhance sales by several times by promoting goods and services to their following, and any businesses that do not utilize this strategy are simply going to lose out on potential growth and possibilities for additional revenue.

You can identify your target market as a social media influencer in a variety of ways. You might decide to check out what your own followers are interested in, or you may decide to see what other people, including the competition in your niche, are posting about on social media to see if it matches your needs and content preferences.

Social Media and Safety

Although influencers on social media might be the hottest thing right now, it is necessary for all who are looking to delve into this profession to be careful. A social media influencer's goals are to grow their audience through their followers, but this is a double-edged sword. The fact that their followers and audience are growing means that there are more people watching them than ever before. There are a number of ways to deal with this; however, there are some best practices you may follow to help you stay safe and secure while influencing on social media. Every social media platform these days comes with security features and settings that you may take advantage of.

These privacy settings are made to keep you safe and to control the amount of private information that you release on social media, as well as to keep others from accessing such information without your consent. You should ideally find out which security options exist in all of the social media websites you decide to use and attempt to understand how to utilize them in the best way. Learn how each function and test them out before you commit to using them. Once you know how everything works and where everything is, you may then make the necessary modifications. You may utilize security tools such as Two-Factor Authentication or biometric security in order to maximize your chances of safety.

You should also consider what you put out on the internet and consider your posts carefully before you publish them. Before you post content, you should ponder on some questions, such as the following:

1. What would I like to accomplish with this post?

2. What do I hope readers will take away from my post?

3. What will other people think of this post?

4. Is this post appropriate for my audience?

5. Does this post reflect who I am?

After answering these questions, you will have eliminated a rather high percentage of any possible bad content that may put you in harm's way. You should also remember to be polite. Being kind to people is crucial. It not only benefits you but others as well. It is possible to inadvertently hurt people with words, especially on social media where there are no physical cues or expressions to fully convey sentiments and contexts. As such, it is rather easy to misinterpret or misjudge something that a person has said. It is common for people to have disagreements. We are human, and conflict is inherently part of our nature. You should try to find common ground and be careful about the things that you say so that you do not offend other people on social media.

There is also the fear of falling for dubious applications and data leaks. As vast as the internet is, there are evildoers and villains who actively seek to exploit others. They sometimes go to extreme lengths, and this could have devastating consequences for an unsuspecting newbie in the social media world. Whenever you are about to install an application on your phone or open up a website on social media, you should first look to verify the page and its authenticity. A seemingly harmless app could have a Trojan virus that steals user information and logs your actions to a file that it sends to its creator. You will need to be mindful of the applications you consume, their properties, and the permissions given to them on your phone.

If you do all of these things and still use social media in a way that is unsafe for your health, then you will ultimately reap no benefits from this book. Just like you need to balance your nutrients from food to gain optimal growth and stamina, you also need to watch your social media intake and usage. Your social media use should not be excessive to the point where it constantly drains your sleep time and causes you to be in a state of constant anxiety or stress. Social media should be fun, and your journey to being an influencer should not be full of unnecessary hardships. You should maintain your social media usage at an average level, and you should also be careful about the kind of content that you consume.

Information can be spread through so many ways, and social media websites and corporations today have been researching how to pass subliminal messages into one's subconscious. This makes it even more pertinent that you keep an eye on the content that you consume. You should ensure that the content showing up on your page is content that you like and relate with, and that this content is safe and okay for consumption.

You shouldn't have to put yourself in harm's way to have a successful social media career. Building your brand, engaging with your audience, and promoting your awesome personality and brand are all things that have been made possible and accessible by the technology of social media. Social media can be used exclusively as a tool to market your brand, goods, or services. You could also use it to develop yourself and produce content that connects with your audience on the social media platform of your choice. Anyone looking to be an influencer such as yourself may grow a following and build an audience on sites such as Facebook, Instagram, YouTube, or X by providing content that piques their interest in their feeds. If all of this is done properly, it can be of enormous help in boosting traffic to websites that offer goods and services, or to any corporations or brands looking to pay for advertising on popular influencers' platforms such as yours.

Valuable Content on Social Media

If you want to get more leads and collaborations as a social media influencer, you will need to share relevant content. It should not just be any kind of content, either. If you want to stimulate people's curiosity and interest, you will need to give them the right kind of information that does that. This book has previously established some tried-and-true methods for producing worthwhile content while creating stunning social media posts that attract the attention of potential clients and customers at the same time.

The secret ingredient in attracting people's attention is content that the audience finds useful. Useful content is organically shared, reposted, rewatched, and used by people. People are more likely to share content that is valuable than to share content that does not serve any purpose whatsoever. When people watch your work and it is relevant and useful to them, they automatically become your marketers and ambassadors. When you provide your audience with value, they are more likely to engage with your business and brand in other ways that are potentially beneficial to you, such as buying your products and goods or patronizing your services.

This kind of situation is beneficial to everyone involved and will increase both your audience as well as your income. By now, you should have learned a couple of useful tricks we have taught you about how to

1. make exciting, useful, and relevant content that users will want to share.

2. write engrossing social media posts that draw in new followers, expand your audience, promote your brand, and find consumers for your product.

3. utilize the power of other influencers and paid advertising to increase your reach and visibility on social media, etc.

By interacting with your audience on social media with relevant, engaging, and useful content, you may use it to generate leads and sales.

Social Media and Branding

The process of building your brand, interacting with potential clients, and earning money with them are all made possible with the power of social media. However, even with the great success stories social media has had, there are still several people who are unaware of how to use social media effectively. To become a productive and successful influencer, one must take steps such as the following:

1. Make a hashtag specific to your brand and use it as much as possible to create high traction.

2. Always use hashtags to link your posts on social media and make them accessible on the internet.

3. Ensure that your hashtags are original, simple to spell, and sourced using digital marketing techniques such as Search Engine Optimization to produce the best results.

4. You should ensure that you have a content strategy and that your content is properly sourced and scheduled. You may make use of any social media tools you like to accomplish this.

5. You should only use the best quality content that you have, and this includes pictures and videos.

6. Ensure you use appropriate images that are sharp and focused, as well as properly lit and edited. Photos that are too dark or light may make you look different than you usually do, so try experimenting till you find the best look.

7. Learn to be original. Utilize various angles and perspectives when you present yourself to your audience so that your

followers may be more interested in all the different parts of your personality and feel more involved.

8. You should always remember that you need other people to succeed and go even farther in your career, so indulge more in working with other influencers. This will help get your name out to the public and can be a wonderful strategy to deploy as a beginner.

9. You could try finding other people who are similar to you in terms of experience and knowledge but also exist in a different niche and try growing with them collectively. For example, if your niche is about cuisine, fine dining, fashion, etc., you could look for people with similar interests but who aren't necessarily part of their own networks yet. Working together will effectively allow you to reach new audiences that would never have been possible otherwise.

10. Post consistently and regularly. Posting regularly is a surefire way to build an audience on social media. Doing this shows your audience that you are serious about your content and committed to your brand. It helps people see how involved you are in the community. It can also let people know what kind of content to anticipate from you as a brand. When people regularly see your content and do not relate to it, it lets them know to stop liking or following your account, leading the way for your content to find its true audience.

Monetizing Your Social Media Influence

The way that we interact with brands and consume content has evolved thanks to the evolution of social media. Social media has become a fantastic method for influencers looking to monetize their large followings or social media platforms. It can, however, be pretty challenging to begin without any prior knowledge. In order to make money off of social media, you should consider the following:

1. **Seek collaborations**: When you first start out monetizing yourself in the social media world, it is critical to develop good

relationships with other brands. These relationships will make the foundation of a good monetary deal between both parties.

2. **Work with trusted companies**: When working with brands, you should work with brands that appeal to you so that there is a connection outside of a working relationship. This way, you can foster and show a genuine willingness to help such a brand succeed. You should exercise caution when selecting your business partners, as you naturally would not want to work with a brand that would ruin your reputation.

3. **Focus on your strengths**: You should think very deeply about this as it goes beyond just your voice and writing style. Consider your distinctive qualities and skills, and think about how you may use them to stand out from the crowd. What are your strengths? How can you best use them? What flaws do you have and how can you develop your strengths to cover them? These are questions you should ask yourself as you ponder your abilities.

4. **Share reliable information**: Sharing authentic information is one of the most important things to do in order to monetize your popularity on social media. Think about the good posts you have seen and what you think makes them better than others. Then try to duplicate that in your own work and your content.

5. **Measure your performance**: In the world of social media, introspection is a great tool. You should always try to look inward and examine your performance. Think about how many people follow you and your number of new followers per day, and try to measure your social media presence and reach.

Now it is about time for you to leave the nest and grow your own wings in this world. Spend some time thinking about what you have read and what you are prepared to do next to make your dream a reality. Questions lie before you, such as who you would follow, who you would share moments with, and what you will share with them. The road is long, and the journey is rocky, but you have the tools and you have the courage.

Admittedly, this is not an easy path to follow. But rest assured that it will be worth it in the end. Social media is such a powerful tool that can help you do a variety of things, including connecting with people, building relationships, developing relationships, and deepening connections. However, this is only possible if you know and understand how to utilize it properly. Our journey so far has revealed that there are many ways to become a social media influencer, as well as many steps that you can take to reach that goal. Hopefully, this book will serve as some inspiration for the road that lies ahead of you. Kindly leave a review to let us know how much you liked this book.

Before you go, we just wanted to say thank you for purchasing our book. You could have picked from dozens of other books on the same topic but you took a chance and chose this one. So, a HUGE thanks to you for getting this book and for reading all the way to the end.

Now, we wanted to ask you for a small favor. COULD YOU PLEASE CONSIDER POSTING A REVIEW ON THE PLATFORM? (Reviews are one of the easiest ways to support the work of independent authors.)

This feedback will help us continue to write the type of books that will help you get the results you want. So if you enjoyed it, please let us know!

We wish you much Success on your Journey!